TOMMY ARMSTRONG

THE PITMAN POET

BY RAY TILLY

GRANDSON OF TOMMY

The proceeds from the sale of this book will be divided between 'The Tommy Armstrong Society' and the North East Region of The Stroke Association.

Front cover: Thomas Armstrong – circa 1890.

Copyright Ray Tilly 2010

First published in 2010 by

Summerhill Books
PO Box 1210
Newcastle-upon-Tyne
NE99 4AH

Email: summerhillbooks@yahoo.co.uk

www.summerhillbooks.co.uk

ISBN: 978-1-906721-30-5

The publisher would like to thank Stanley historian, Jack Hair for his help with the publication of this book.

CONTENTS

ACKNOWLEDGEMENTS

I am indebted to many people and organisations, without whose help this book could not have been completed so I would like to express my gratitude to all of them.

Margaret A.E. Tilly – my mother. Whilst she has not contributed directly to the content of the book, she gave me love, care and encouragement in everything I did, right up to the time of her death in 1977.

Elizabeth Hawkings – a dear friend of my mother who gave me the breakthrough with the identity of my father, William Hunter Armstrong and Jack Mains who re-introduced me to Elizabeth.

Paul Armstrong – Paul kindly participated in a DNA comparison with me to confirm that his known great grandfather, William Hunter Armstrong, was my father.

Judith Anne Murphy and her excellent dissertation of 2003 entitled 'Heritage & Harmony' which contained a chapter specific to Tommy Armstrong. Judith kindly gave me permission to use any of the content of her dissertation.

Rosemary Allan and the Beamish Regional Resource Centre which holds much material relating to the area and specifically to Tommy Armstrong. The Resource Centre kindly approved my use of any of its relevant material including photographs.

Ross Forbes – Editor of *Polisses & Candymen: The Complete Works of Tommy Armstrong, The Pitman Poet*. Ross kindly allowed me to use any of the content of the book.

Gerald Ash (Chairman) and Joe Wilson (Secretary) of the Tommy Armstrong Society which they formed in 2006.

George Nairn of Chester-le-Street who kindly supplied me with and allowed me to use many of the photographs which appear in this book.

Anne Armstrong – whose grandfather had lived in the same household as Tommy Armstrong and knew him well. What Anne learnt about Tommy from her grandfather she was pleased to share with me.

Katherine Beaumont – the widow of Alec Moir who was the stepson of William Hunter Armstrong. Katherine learnt a lot about Alec's stepfather which she kindly shared with me.

Ivan Garnham – a retired Headmaster of Tanfield Lea Junior School who knew William Hunter Armstrong well and kindly shared his memories with me.

Mr & Mrs Roe and Mr & Mrs Nunn of the village of Tanfield Lea who were pleased to tell me about their recollections of my father.

The Special Collections Section of the Library at Goldsmiths College, London which holds a Collection of the Folklorist, A.L. Lloyd. The Collection contains notes and writings relating to Tommy Armstrong and his son William Hunter Armstrong.

Ruth S. Nicholson (my daughter) who translated an article by A.L. Lloyd from German to English so that I could read it.

Mr Frank Manders of Sunderland for his knowledge of the history of The Star Picture Hall, Tantobie.

The Newspaper Library Section of the British Library which holds a wonderful collection of 19th and 20th century national and regional newspapers.

Durham County Record Office and Tyne & Wear Archives Service, both of which hold many and various records which have been most helpful during my research.

Nick Townsend and Mike Grassly for their advice and recommendations on the construction of this book.

To discover the identity of my father, William Hunter Armstrong and grandfather, Thomas Armstrong has been an exciting adventure for me. As I progressed, I discovered a number of new relatives and have met many of them. They have all welcomed me into the fold of the Armstrong family and have given as much help as they can with my research. They are:

Descendants of Tommy Armstrong: Alan Armstrong, his sister Joan and his son Paul; David Horsley; Jean Coffell and her brothers Dennis & Kenneth Armstrong.

Descendants of Tommy's brother William Wilson Armstrong: William Armstrong Hall, his wife Darryl & their son Timothy; Diane Ward & her husband John.

Descendants of Tommy's brother Henry Armstrong: Anne Armstrong; Cecil Winston Armstrong; Elizabeth Armstrong Marshall.

THE AUTHOR

Ray Tilly was born in 1934 at Eighton Banks, County Durham the illegitimate son of Margaret A.E. Tilly. He attended Chester-le-Street Grammar School then after eighteen months as a Police Cadet in Durham Constabulary, enlisted into the Army and was stationed at Windsor.

Upon his discharge from the Army, he stayed in the south and joined the Police Service, rising to the rank of Chief Superintendent before retiring from Thames Valley Police in 1985 and settling in Buckinghamshire.

He then worked as a Security Consultant until completely retiring in 2002. Since then, he has been engaged with researching family history which led to learning the identity of his father and hence the desire to write this book.

INTRODUCTION

The North East has produced many notable sons but one who can take his rightful place in the culture and history of the area is Tommy Armstrong, The Pitman Poet of Tanfield Lea. A remarkable character, his writings embrace the hardship and humour of West Durham mining life during the 1800s and early 1900s.

However, he was reputedly a drunkard and a thief whereas his son, William Hunter Armstrong, was a moral upstanding figure in the local community. The question is, are these statements accurate? As these two people are my father and grandfather, I needed to know the answer so I have used my thirty years experience as a police officer, mainly as a detective, to investigate their lives. In my view, there have been misconceptions about both men so by publishing this book I hope to set the record straight.

As the illegitimate son of Margaret A.E. Tilly (Maggie) who never married, I was raised by my mother and her parents in the village of Eighton Banks, County Durham where my mother was deeply involved with the Primitive Methodist Church. In 1943, at the age of nine and after my grandparents died, my mother and I moved to Birtley to live with Mr & Mrs Dawson who owned a shop where my mother worked. Having had a loving and caring upbringing by my mother and grandparents, then living in a happy family environment with Mr & Mrs Dawson, I never had any concern about there not being a father around.

Jubilee Avenue Primitive Methodist Church, Eighton Banks.

On one occasion whilst on leave from the Army, my mother raised the subject but not wanting her to upset herself, I stopped the conversation. She did say that the man concerned had later made another lady pregnant and had married her. That was the extent of the conversation; no names or places.

In the year 2000, I took up family history research and in 2006, curiosity prompted me to wonder if it might be possible to establish the identity of my father. By this time of course, all my relatives who could have given any positive help had died. The only lead I could get was from a cousin who had been told that my father was connected with the Methodist Church. Because of my mother's involvement with the church, this was not really surprising but considerable research of church records failed to produce any likely candidate as my father.

I learnt of a lady in Kent who was a native of Eighton Banks and had written an article about Methodism in the village so I wrote to her with my quest. She herself was not able to help but she pointed me in the direction of Jack Mains, who is a few years older than me and Elizabeth Hawkings (nee Gault), who is nineteen years older than me. I remembered both of them from the time I lived at Eighton Banks, particularly Elizabeth who I often used to visit with my mother, so I made contact with Jack who re-introduced me to Elizabeth who is known as Betsy.

Betsy Hawkings gave me the breakthrough that I needed. She knew my father who was a member of 'The Order of the Sons of Temperance Society' (SOT). Betsy and my mother were also members of SOT and used to meet my father when they attended meetings at Newcastle upon Tyne. The friendship between my father and mother developed when she used to help care for his second wife who was wheelchair bound at their home in Tanfield Lea. Armed with this fantastic information from Betsy, I researched SOT and other records then visited Tanfield Lea.

After that, matters moved on quite quickly and I was thrilled to meet descendants from my father's first marriage and other relatives. When I decided to embark on writing this book, I realised that whilst I was satisfied from all I had learnt that I was the son of William Hunter Armstrong, others might query it. To avoid any future dispute, a comparison of DNA samples from me and Paul Armstrong, the known great grandson of William Hunter Armstrong, confirmed the fact.

I keep in contact with Betsy Hawkings, now aged ninety five (2010) who is always a pleasure to meet and we reminisce about Eighton Banks. I also maintain contact with Paul Armstrong and his lovely family. Thanks to their help, I have now found and met some wonderful relatives and made many new friends in County Durham.

Having identified my father, it was easy and very exciting to identify my grandfather as Thomas Armstrong (1848-1920), who was a poet in the Durham Coalfield and well known as Tommy Armstrong, The Pitman Poet of Tanfield Lea. However, it came as a shock to learn that Tommy was supposed to have been a drunkard and spent six months in

Durham Jail for stealing. More surprise followed when I learnt that the first recorded suggestion of Tommy's incarceration came from his own son (my father) in 1951, which was *thirty one* years after Tommy's death!

It is not therefore surprising that after 1951, publications about Tommy feature the story of him spending six months in Durham Jail and even embellish the circumstances. After all, scandal about a well known character makes more exciting reading than a typical working man's life of the day. Tommy certainly wrote a poem entitled 'Durham Jail' but it does not mean that he himself spent time inside. The content of the poem about what went on inside the jail would have been fairly common knowledge. So we are left with the situation that up to now, books and television programmes have portrayed Tommy as a drunkard and a thief.

My grandfather Tommy, spent all his working life in the coal mines but unfortunately, there are no Personnel Records for either the period or the collieries in which he is likely to have worked. The most certain information about Tommy is that which is obtainable from Certificates of Birth, Marriage & Death, Census Returns, Parish Registers and other similar records. The next most reliable sources are newspapers containing reports on factual events or correspondence from Tommy himself. We are then left with what other people have written or said about Tommy, some of which needs to be treated with care.

At an early age, Tommy started writing poems, many of which were put to music and are still sung today by Folk Groups in the North East of England. Many of his works were written in local dialect but those likely to be read by a wider audience, were written in standard English, eg. 'The Trimdon Grange Explosion'. He has written poems that have never been published, some of which may have been lost forever. This book contains a compilation of all Tommy's works that have been published

23 Jubilee Avenue, Eighton Banks. Home of Margaret A.E. Tilly and where her son Ray Tilly was born.

plus some that have not previously been published.

My father William, lived most of his life in Tanfield Lea and he too spent all his working life in the coal mines, most likely Tanfield Lea Colliery. Information about William comes from the same sources as described for Tommy plus records of involvement with the National Union of Mineworkers, various societies and the church. Like his father before him, he had an interest in poetry and in the village was known as 'Poety' but he was not such a prolific poetry writer as Tommy.

There is no doubt that both were good men in their different ways and gave much to the lives of others around them but questions arise about each of them.

Was Thomas Armstrong the drunkard and criminal he is alleged to have been? And was his son William Hunter Armstrong the completely moral, upstanding figure in his community that we understand from contemporary reports of the time?

In the light of new research and by delving deeper into the lives of this father and son, it is the aim of this book to set the record straight and to publish all the known works of both men. Throughout the book, Thomas Armstrong is referred to as 'Tommy' and William Hunter Armstrong is referred to as 'WHA'.

Ray Tilly

Dedication

This book is dedicated to my wife Marigold and my children Ruth, Helen, Elizabeth and Graham.

I am indebted to my wife Marigold for many reasons. Firstly for her tolerance of my months of 'solitary confinement' when I was trying to put words to paper. Next for her personal help with research at various repositories, particularly the British Library Newspaper Reading Room in North London where we have spent many happy weeks trawling through old newspapers.

Finally, for her love, encouragement and understanding of my desire to write this book.

PART ONE

THOMAS ARMSTRONG
(1848 – 1920)

Tommy Armstrong (seated) and three friends outside the Oak Tree Inn, Tantobie – circa 1912.

Chapter 1
WHO WAS TOMMY?

Tommy Armstrong was a little man with a big heart. He was a coal miner in the North West Durham Coalfield and spent all his working life in coal mines in and around Tanfield Lea from the age of about nine years, until his early sixties when ill health forced him to retire.

From an early age, probably fifteen, he started writing poetry and soon became renowned in the area for his humour and ability to entertain. It was not long before he and fellow artistes were performing at concerts to raise money for charitable purposes, such as to help the injured or bereaved in mining accidents. Some of his works were printed and sold at a penny a time with the proceeds going to benefit the bereaved or needy. One of his best known poems is 'The Trimdon Grange Explosion' which is about that disaster when 74 men and boys were killed in 1882. Another well known poem based on an actual event, is 'The Durham Strike' which refers to the time when the whole workforce of Durham Coalfield was 'locked out' in 1892.

Tommy knew what it was to hear the disaster siren ringing in his ears. He would then think up ballads and include reference to dead men in whose company he had probably been the day before.

Other writings were total imagination on his part. 'Marla Hill Ducks' was about twenty ducks that were arrested for trespassing and put into 'Marla Hill Jail'. 'Th' Row Between Th' Caiges' was about a new lift cage and an old lift cage operating alongside each other in a pit shaft; they got arguing and eventually fighting to decide which of them was the best. This was Tommy being creative.

Tommy Armstrong was probably the best workers' song writer in his time and is ranked amongst other song writers such as George Ridley who wrote 'Blaydon Races' and 'Cushie Butterfield' and Joe Wilson who wrote 'Keep Your Feet Still Geordie Hinny'.

There are only two known existing photographs of Tommy. The one on the front cover of this book (circa 1890) and the other one on the previous page where he is with three friends outside the 'Oak Tree Inn' at Tantobie (circa 1912). This is where Tommy used to write some of his works.

BIRTH, PARENTS AND EDUCATION

"I was born at Shotley Bridge, I've heard my mother say; 'Twas in the month of August and on the fifteenth day." These were the first lines of two verses Tommy included at the end of a letter he wrote to the Editor of the local newspaper in 1917[1]. They were written in standard English and in that respect, contrast with the original poem which Tommy wrote in dialect and named "Th' Borth E Th' Lad". In the letter to the Editor, Tommy said he intended to have a ride to Shotley Bridge to have a look at number seventeen, the cottage where he was born. It is known from his Birth Certificate that he was born on the 15th August

Shotley Bridge where Tommy was born in 1848.

1848 in Wood Street, Shotley Bridge but the Certificate does not give the number of the house so Tommy himself has been kind enough to identify the number as seventeen. In 1851, Tommy was still living there with his parents and two of his brothers[2]. His younger brother Henry, as well as being the nearest to Tommy by age, was the nearest in friendship and they remained close friends until the time Tommy died in 1920.

Tommy was born during the reign of Queen Victoria and the Prime Minister was Lord Russell (Liberal). Capital Punishment in the form of 'public hanging' was still performed until 1865 when Tommy was aged seventeen. When Tommy died, King George V was on the throne and David Lloyd George (Coalition) was Prime Minister.

Tommy's father, Timothy Armstrong, was born at Hamsterley, County Durham in 1815[3] and his mother Mary (nee Wilson) was born at Wigton, Cumberland in 1820[4]. They met whilst both were living at Haswell, married in 1842[5], then moved to Shotley Bridge. They had five children: William, Thomas, Henry, Mary and Timothy (See Page 179 for the Family Tree).

Two hours schooling each day for children became compulsory in 1833 but it was not until 1870 that full time education became compulsory for children aged five to twelve[6]. There is no doubt that Tommy took advantage of what tuition was available in the three Rs (Reading, wRiting and aRithmetic), probably from 1853 to 1857. His ability to read is evident from some of his works which were written after reading newspaper reports on the subject matter, as in "Trimdon Grange Explosion". His ability to write is evident from the numerous letters he wrote to local newspapers using good grammar, whether in dialect or standard English. His ability with numbers is evident from some works he wrote that certainly involved arithmetic, such as "The Prudent Pitman".

WORKING LIFE

Claims differ as to where and when Tommy worked. His son WHA, stated that Tommy first worked down the mine at East Tanfield Colliery aged nine[7], whereas, an article in a local newspaper in 1914 claimed he started work in the Medomsley Busty Pit aged eight[8]. WHA went on to say that Tommy spent all his working life in Tanfield Moor, Tanfield Lea and East Tanfield Collieries working for Joicey & Co[7]. In contradiction of this, a local author states that Tommy spent much of his working life at West Shield Row Colliery, known locally as 'Oakey's Pit' because it was originally owned by a Mr Charles Edward Oakey[9]. In 1920, a local newspaper published a letter from Tommy's close brother Henry, with recollections of Tommy following his death. In it, Henry stated that in 1866, Tommy with his three brothers moved to East Tanfield Colliery where Tommy worked for a number of years[10]. This move to East Tanfield must have been towards the end of 1866 because it is known from fortnightly pay bills that Tommy and his older brother William, were hewers in the Brockwell Seam at Addison Pit until the end of September 1866[11].

One thing certain is that wherever Tommy worked and all during his

A 'Trapper Boy' circa 1910 but this was long after Tommy would have worked in that role.

working life underground, coal mining was a dangerous occupation. Mining disasters often took place resulting in many deaths and injury. Risks came from various sources including floods, roof collapse and explosion. Working conditions were terrible; confined space underground, dirty work with no pit baths, the risk of disease such as lung infection and the ever present risk of accident.

The Coal Mines Act 1842 made it illegal to employ females of any age and boys below the age of ten, underground. However, it was many years before the provisions of the Act were enforced so it is very likely that Tommy did start work underground before reaching the age of ten. His first job underground would have been that of a 'Trapper Boy' which was to sit beside a wooden door and by use of a rope, open and close the door to allow people or coal tubs to pass through. This was to assist with the circulation of air and to reduce the risk of explosion. The usual progress from a 'Trapper Boy' was to a 'Pony Driver' leading a pony pulling tubs of coal, then to a 'Putter' who supplied the 'Hewer' with tubs, then eventually to a 'Hewer' who worked at the coal face with a hand held pick. His job was to produce good pieces of coal.

The only known roles of Tommy whilst he worked in the coal mines are what have been learnt from official records. In 1866 at Addison Colliery, he was first a Putter then a Hewer with his older brother William[11]. When the Census was taken in 1901, he was shown as a 'Coal Worker Underground'. On most other Certificates and Census Returns he was shown as either a miner or coal miner which was generally the case for all categories of mine worker. On his own Death Certificate, he was shown as a 'Retired Colliery Shifter' which was a man paid so much per shift and usually employed on repair work.

In 1951, WHA claimed that his father Tommy, " … was just over five feet tall and very bow legged, caused through pains, in fact his eldest brother had to take him to the pit on his back."[7] This is the first time any reference can be found to Tommy being carried on his brother's back. Tommy's close brother Henry, never referred to it in his recollections of Tommy, nor did any other correspondents who wrote to local newspapers with reminiscences of Tommy. Surely such circumstances would have prompted comments from others during the life of Tommy and would also have been good material for a poem from Tommy himself. It is presumed that for whatever reason, the story from WHA is a myth which has been perpetuated and enhanced by some authors and narrators of stories about Tommy. After all, it makes a good story.

From when Tommy commenced work about 1857, he would have been subject to the hated 'Miner's Bond' until it was abolished in 1872. The Bond, which was entered into at the beginning of April, contracted the miners to a 'Master' (Colliery Owner) for a year. If miners broke the terms of the Bond, they were liable to arrest, trial and imprisonment. The annual 'Bonding' allowed 'Masters' to pick and choose from existing and potential employees, so disposing of troublemakers or shirkers. It was also the only time in the year when miners could lawfully leave one employer and move to another where wages, conditions or housing might be slightly better. As married miners lived in tied cottages, the annual 'Bonding' was a time when lots of families took to the road moving from one pit village to another. There is no doubt that the Bond was heavily loaded in favour of the Colliery Owners and tied the mineworkers as virtual slaves[12].

Hewer working at the coal face.

MARRIAGES AND CHILDREN

On Christmas Day 1869, Tommy married Mary Ann Hunter at Gateshead Register Office. The Marriage Certificate shows Mary's age as twenty-one but this is not right. She was only sixteen, having been born at Tanfield Lea on the 30th May 1853. The reason for giving the wrong age is not known but she clearly had parental consent because her father was a witness to the marriage. Tommy and Mary had a total of fourteen children, six boys and eight girls. Sadly, eight children died young so only six (three boys and three girls) reached adulthood and married. (See Page 179 for the Family Tree)

Tommy's wife Mary died in 1898 when only aged 44 years, leaving Tommy with two working sons and three younger children still at home. Tommy took on three housekeepers in succession but none proved satisfactory, so he kept his eldest daughter Margaret away from school to keep house. This resulted in Tommy appearing in front of Tanfield School Board as shown in the funny report in the *Consett Chronicle* on Friday 11th May 1900 which reads as follows:

TANFIELD SCHOOL BOARD

The monthly meeting of this Board was held on Tuesday night, the members present being – Mr H.C. Wood (presiding), Rev. T.H. Archdall, Mr J. Green, Mr W. Bulmer, Mr B. Mason, Rev. J. Thompson, Mr W. Severs, Mr G. Armstrong, Mr S. Meddick (Attendance Officer) and Mr W.H. Ritson (Clerk).

THE TANFIELD POET AND WOMEN

Mr Thomas Armstrong, the well known poet of Tanfield Lea, applied to the Board to have his twelve year old daughter exempted from attendance at school. He explained his circumstances, his wife being dead and he having a family of five. He added that he was going to have no more women-folk in the house, unless he got them made at the brick flats. (Laughter). He had had three since his wife died and they were all deceivers.

THE CHAIRMAN remarked that he did not know women were made at the brick flats. Mr Meddick said that the remainder of Mr Armstrong's family were regular in their attendances and this girl had been during the time Mr Armstrong had had a housekeeper.

On the motion of Mr SEVERS, seconded by Mr ARCHDALL, it was decided to grant the application. Mr BULMER suggested that Mr Armstrong should allow his daughter to attend the evening school at Tanfield Lea in the winter months and Mr Armstrong expressed his willingness to do so. He further intimated, amid much laughter, that if he got married again he would send his daughter to school again but he would let all the members know of this by sending them an invitation to attend the wedding tea.

In another part of the same newspaper appeared the following funny article relating to the event:

A POET AND THE WOMEN-FOLK

Poets are popularly supposed to be tender, sympathetic, loveable, impressionable beings. But Tommy Armstrong, the Tanfield Poet, is not the man to be carried away by that kind of sentimental nonsense. He reckons up the women-folk and finds that they are all deceivers. That was the conclusion that another Tommy, the Willington Weather Prophet, came to after the loss of his first spouse. Since the death of his first love, the Tanfield Poet has had three housekeepers, not one of whom was fit to tie her shoe-strings. They turned out such a bad lot that he has decided to dispense with a housekeeper altogether, unless he can get one made at the brick flats. This decision he communicated to the Tanfield School Board on Tuesday evening. The Chairman, Mr Wood, seemed surprised that the human form divine could be supplied to order at a brickmaking establishment. This only goes to show how ignorant we sometimes are of our everyday surroundings. Surely the Chairman of the Tanfield School Board must have heard of such a thing as a "Clay Dolly." It is the possession of one of these that the Tanfield Poet yearns for. The least the Board can do is to help him get one. If, after his wish is gratified, it does not come up to his expectations, he can hand it over to William, or, better still, it might be rocked to sleep in the cradle upstairs!

At Tanfield Parish Church on the 9th February 1901, Tommy married Ann Thompson, a Widow. The marriage was referred to in the *Consett Chronicle* in a Column which contained snippets of information and reads:

WE KNOW

That the Tanfield Poet has forsaken the vow made to the School Board and has taken at the same time, a new vow and a new better half.

Tanfield Parish Church.

It is assumed that this second marriage did not work out because in 1911, Tommy was living with his widowed daughter Mary Robson and her children in Tanfield Lea[13]. At the same time, his wife Ann was living with her married daughter, Dorothy Proctor and her family at Pelton Fell[14]. When Ann died in 1918, she was living with another married daughter, Sarah Elizabeth Nation and her family at Chester-le-Street[15].

THE QUOITS PLAYER

In 1924, a series of three articles, each headed 'POPULAR PASTIMES' was published in a local newspaper[16]. These had been written by Tommy's close brother Henry Armstrong and published after the death of Henry. They related to the game Quoits which was very popular in the North East of England during the 19th century.

Henry Armstrong explained how he and Tommy were watching a Quoits match early in 1864 when Tommy, who was aged only fifteen, realised how to overcome an advantage held by an opponent. Tommy and Henry went home and practised what became known as 'Round Hand Playing'. Tommy first played in public at Leadgate, pitching his new style in a handicap when aged only sixteen. He was a surprise to the older men and by his intuition, added much to the skill of the game. Other men started to play 'Round Handed' which improved their standard of play considerably.

Men used to play for large stakes which could be as much as £100 and in the 1870s that was a lot of money. Henry referred to a match between Tommy and Philip Allan of West Pelton for the sum of £80 but omitted to mention who won. He also referred to Tommy playing for £40 and £50 as a regular occurrence.

From 1872 to 1880, quoits playing made its greatest progress as a game of skill in West Durham and many men, including Tommy, became very proficient in the game at ten yards. Luke Dodds, himself a good player, had a public house at Shield Row where he had a Quoits Pitch made. Men from all parts of the district used to play there and Tommy was often to be found playing matches at the ground. After playing a match, Tommy would often entertain the company at night by giving details of the contest and the participants in rhyme[17].

A quoits pitch consisted of two 3 feet squares of clay, eleven yards apart, each with a hob (iron post) in the centre which protruded three inches above the surface. The quoits were circular pieces of iron with a hole in the middle, about six inches in diameter and weighing about $5^1/_2$ pounds. The game was played by opposing players pitching two quoits from one end with a view to landing over the hob (a ringer) or as near as possible to it. The maximum score for each end was two points and the first player to reach 21 was the winner. A ringer scored two points but if there was more than one ringer, only the top one scored. A quoit touching the hob scored one point. If all four quoits missed the hob, a single point went to the opponent with the quoit nearest to the hob.

Three Quoits Players.

Chapter 2
THE POET

Tommy wrote poems on a variety of themes. He wrote to entertain and make people laugh, as he did with 'The Cat Pie'. He wrote to castigate the colliery owners, especially at times of lockouts, an example being 'Durham Strike'. He wrote to ridicule those who abused their authority such as in 'Oakey's Keeker'. He wrote to appreciate the kindness of others as shown in 'Old Folks Tea'. Most important of all, he wrote about tragedies which occurred in coal mines or elsewhere, perhaps the best known being 'Trimdon Grange Explosion'.

Trimdon Grange Colliery.

As far as can be determined, Tommy wrote his first poem in 1864 when aged sixteen and called it 'Th' Borth E Th' Lad' in which he describes his own birth. Like many of his poems, it was written in dialect and after each of the four verses, he added a paragraph to be spoken. This was a method he also adopted with some of his later works. It was said that Tommy himself could not sing but he wrote many of his works as songs and directed the tune to which they should be sung. 'Castles In The Air' was a tune he often chose. Evidence of his early writing, his willingness to help others and his inability to sing is to be found in the following letter published in the local newspaper in 1916[1]. The letter gives a flavour of the character of Tommy and his desire to help those in need.

TOMMY ARMSTRONG
REMINISCENCES OF A FAMOUS TANFIELD SONG WRITER
BY AN ACQUAINTANCE

"A week or two ago a correspondent to the "Consett and Stanley Chronicle" (Mr Allison) for a long time resident in North West Durham, asked and was correctly informed as to the authorship of the well-known and popular Tyneside song, "Nanny's a Mazer." Tommy Armstrong of Tanfield was the author. Mr Allison's reference to the days when he heard Tommy recite some of his poetry at Dipton Hall revives old memories and as one who has known Tommy all his life, I would like to say a few things that may be of interest to your readers.

Tommy came to live at South Pontop in the year 1864 and it was in that year he composed his first song. Like most of his songs, it had in it some incident that had just taken place. Right through his compositions, this principle is to be found. Well, his first attempt was tried on an Annfield Plain soiree. Those were the occasions for which much effort was made to raise money – teas, concerts and balls, in order to raise money for Reading Rooms, etc. Tommy was at his first soiree in this year and he was closely interested in this concert and the artistes who had the platform. There was Mr McMillan, a comic very popular in the district at that time and Joe Wilson who was making his name as a singer of Tyneside songs. Tommy wrote some verses describing the singing on that occasion but the song was never printed. He tells us that:-

> First McMillan sung and he sung see funny and queer;
> Then Joe Wilson sung his song, "Aa wish yor feyther was here."
> After he'd sung that see well he sang "Geordy haad the bairn;"
> He caused the women folk to feel, with the wax doll in his arm.

> Then McMillan he sung agyn, the funniest of the lot;
> Aboot the Englishman and Scotsman and what the Paddy got.
> They everyone had dreamt a dream but Paddy had them off;
> For he dreamt while they were sleeping he up and eat the loaf.

Tommy began to turn his attention to the incidents of the daily life and to extract humour from them in his own quaint phraseology. The same year, I am told:-

> Says Lumley's wife ter Mrs Gray, "Ye should be turned about;"
> Ye're never out the house the day the gutter's to be cleaned out.
> Says Mrs Gray to Lumley's wife, "Ye'd better haad yer jaw;
> You hev more gob about the gutter than all the blooming raa"

> Now the row had just begun when Mrs Carrol came out;
> She says, "Aam missen aal the fun, what's aal the noise about?"
> Said Mrs Gray to Mrs Carrol, "Aa waarned ye're in a splutter;
> Ye've nowt ter dee with the row at aal, it's just about the gutter."

And so the row went on with all the neighbours fighting to the great joy of Tommy and his youthful companions.

It was not until the year of 1870 that he became famous in this district as a special entertainer and he began to receive invitations to sing at concerts arranged for charitable purposes, institutes and any cause that had need of funds and his services were readily at their disposal. He was not a singer, neither did he profess to be but when his name appeared on a bill, that concert was a certain success and many a widow and working man in low water owed something to Tommy who when he knew, would raise a concert to help his fellow men or women to rise above penury and want.

He knew nothing of music and was often a puzzle to the musician playing for him. Once, when he was singing at a benefit concert and he was late in coming on to sing and when his turn did come on, the pianist came to him to get the key of his song and music. "What is your key Mr Armstrong?" enquired the pianist. "Oh, the bed key is my key. Sit thee way doon there until aw come back. I'll manage without thoo."

It was his spontaneous wit that made him so popular among his own and other people. I have known him come on to the platform and stand a minute or two and never speak and the people would be cracking their side with laughter, knowing full well they would get something new. There was one thing that helped him very much. He never broke down while singing a song by forgetting a verse or two. His gift for extempore verse covered his defeat.

Perhaps it will be safe to say that in the position of chairman he showed to best advantage. When dressed in a long top coat and false whiskers he made a splendid disguise and to know him when he had thrown this garb away used to make more fun than many funny songs. At this time, Tommy had a troupe of very good talent. One was Tommy Gray, a good singer of Tyneside and other local songs. Gray won a gold medal given by Mr Christopher Barrass, proprietor of The Oxford, Newcastle for the best Pitman Singer of Northumberland and County Durham. Tommy sang Tommy Armstrong's songs and won with his last song, 'Durham Jail.' Another very popular member was James McDonald of Tanfield Lea, a favourite Irish comic with good voice and deportment. William McCrum, another comic was always well received. He was a good dancer and always willing to give his services. There was also John Jackson of Dipton, comic singer who was always well taken with at any concert he lent his services to and with old Tommy among them, you could be sure of a merry time at any concert.

To hear Mr McCrum and Tommy Armstrong sing 'The Unhappy Couple' was delightful. If you were in the dumps when they commenced, your bad temper was soon gone. No one could resist laughing. It was no uncommon thing to hear both men and women exclaim, gasping for breath, "Oh dear me. Oh dear me." Fun was this troupe's object. Like Harry Lauder, they were out to make men and women laugh. They had many enquiries for their services and being of generous turn of mind, they had plenty of engagements. They always gave their services free to help the weak, let it be Society or individual.

I remember at this time, a much respected resident of Annfield Plain needed a friend to assist him. His friends in that village arranged for a concert to help and engaged some artistes from Newcastle to give the concert. When it was all paid for, there was no help for the needy man; the artistes took away the lion's share. This led the friends of the poor man to come to Tommy to see if he and his troupe would give them a concert. They agreed to go and even paid for the printing of the bills themselves. The Annfield Plain Store very kindly allowed use of the Store Hall free. The concert came off quite a success. The people could not all get in and many were standing out to the top of the stairs from the hall. Tommy acted as chairman, wearing his false whiskers and long coat to cover his not over straight legs. Scarcely anyone but his near friends knew who the chairman was until half time, when it was announced that the chairman and one of his children would sing 'The School Board Man,' and when Tommy came on to the stage minus his whiskers and top coat, the roars of laughter were tremendous. The song was a treat and received much applause. But when Tommy appeared again in the top coat and whiskers, it is impossible to describe the noise.

He did these things to make people laugh and enjoy themselves and incidentally, to materially assist a poor brother struggling along life's uneven pathway. Now in his old and infirm age, he can look back with pride and consolation and with the knowledge that he made it easier for someone to live."

The Annfield Plain Co-operative Store.

No trace can be found of any of the contents of the above letter having been reported in any newspaper or written in any other publication prior to 1916. They were certainly published in the 1950s onwards and some authors even repeated the stories verbatim.

The two verses about the women arguing read as if they should be part of Tommy's poem, 'Th' Row I' Th' Gutter' but they do not feature as such. Whether they were part of the original poem which Tommy later amended will never be known.

The same author wrote another letter which was published in the newspaper shortly afterwards, the first part of which reads as follows[2]:-

TOMMY ARMSTRONG
FURTHER REMINISCENCES OF VETERAN TANFIELD POET
(BY ONE WHO KNOWS HIM)

"In my last article concerning Thomas Armstrong of Tanfield, 'Tommy the Poet' as he is widely known, I outlined the part he played on the platform of North West Durham. As a topical rhymester, Tommy was unique. His rugged poems in the vernacular were delightfully original, as for instance 'Wor Nanny's a Mazor' and 'Aa wish me feyther was heeor,' amusing examples in the Tyneside twang which were sung to catchy tunes. Some particulars of how Tommy came to write many of his ever popular songs over forty years ago will be interesting.

Over forty years ago, there was at Shield Row, a set of young men who made a practice of going to a certain house on Sunday afternoons after the public houses had closed and often eat what meat was left from Coxon's dinner. But this man contrived once to get a cat-meat pie and when his company arrived, they were induced to steal the pie. They ran off with their prize and enjoyed themselves with the limbs of a cat. Joe Peel got a leg which he thought was enough. He said, "Man it's nice but it's awfully teuf." It was a common thing to hear those men mewing at each other in the public houses, after 'the cat had been let out of the bag' as a reminder of the joke played upon them by J. Coxon and Bob Charlton.

Again, we have the song on 'The Cleaning of the Gutter,' the open channels which were often the scene of much fighting among the women who happened to live in the street where there was an open channel. Tommy depicts one of these splendid displays of arms such as pokers, long tongues, family secrets and all kinds of useful ammunition which was always plentiful on occasions like these.
He says:

> They sent for the doctor; his name was John Proctor.
> And then for the Pollisses – Jackson and Jones.
> An' they sent a letter for Hall the bone-setter;
> An' it took him three days for to set aal their bones."

These lines are part of the last verse of Tommy's poem, 'Th' Row I' Th' Gutter' so whether he initially called the poem 'The Cleaning of the Gutter', will never be known.

Again, the contents of this letter were never seen prior to 1916 but from the 1950s onwards, they have been used by authors, sometimes verbatim.

The earliest newspaper report of Tommy performing in public was in 1869 and reads as follows[3]:

STANLEY PENNY READINGS

"The fortnightly penny readings in connection with the Stanley Reading-room and Library took place in the Infant School-room on Wednesday evening with Mr T.W. Ritson, secretary, presiding. Mr M. Stewart sang some Scottish songs in good taste and Mr J. Armstrong's readings were well received, as also was the reading of Mr Wm. Fitzpatrick.

Mr Thomas Armstrong however, appeared to be the "man of the hour." His local songs, "Stanley Reading Room" and "The Tanfield Brake" provoked a perfect storm of merriment, as all the hits were so apposite and the characters introduced were so well known. There was a large attendance and an interesting evening was spent."

This article mentions two of Tommy's songs. One was 'The Tanfield Brake' which is one of his well known published works. The other was 'Stanley Reading Room' which has not been published and of which no trace can be found. It is assumed therefore that this is one of his works which may have disappeared forever.

A pamphlet is said to have been published in 1914 of Tommy's composition entitled, 'Me Aud Songs' but no trace of it can be found[4]. It is said to contain the following which has been repeated by numerous authors since 1951: "When ye're the Pitman's Poet an' looked up to for it, wey, if a disaster or a strike or a murder goes by wi'oot a sang fre ye, the' say: What's the matter wi' Tommy Armstrong? Has somebody druv a spigot in him an' let oot a' the inspiration? Me aad sangs hev kept me in beer, an' the floor o' the public bar hes bin me stage for forty years. Aw'd sing, we'd drink, aw'd sing, we'd drink agen, sangs wi'oot end, amen."

A.L. Lloyd (1908-1982), a highly acclaimed and internationally known Folklorist, admired the works of Tommy. Knowing about Tommy as a poet, Lloyd had visited the village of Tanfield Lea to learn a little about Tommy as a man. In 1964, Lloyd wrote an article for a German Folklore Journal about the development of political songwriting[5]. The main theme of the article concerned Tommy about whom he said, "We are concerned here with one of the most remarkable creators of English worker's song, Tommy Armstrong from Durham. He was a poor but talented songwriter." Lloyd went on to further compliment the ability of Tommy and verses from six of Tommy's works were featured in the article. To receive praise of this nature from a Folklorist of such high standing clearly shows that Tommy was indeed a gifted and talented poet.

At the end of this book is a compilation of all the works of Tommy that have been traced – 46 in all. They consist of 30 that have often been published or sung plus six which are known to the Beamish Regional Resource Centre that have not been previously published. In addition, there are ten of his works which have been found in old newspapers and have not been previously published elsewhere.

CHARITABLE WORK

Tommy did much for the benefit of those who suffered from pit disasters or other misfortune. To indicate Tommy's kindness and willingness to help others in their time of need, some examples of his charitable work are shown in this chapter.

In 1873, a local newspaper reported on a grand concert held in the Tanfield Infant School Room for the benefit of Joseph Thirlaway, who had been 'unable to follow his employment for two years through affliction'. Tommy officiated as chairman and as well as calling upon various artistes, he sang 'The Derwent Valley Collision' which caused much merriment and laughter. Sadly, Joseph Thirlaway who had been a coal miner, died at Tanfield in April 1874 at the young age of twenty eight[6]. Unfortunately, no trace can be found of 'The Derwent Valley Collision' so it might be another of Tommy's works that has been lost forever.

In 1878, another newspaper report told of a concert held in the room of Dipton Co-operative Society, on behalf of the widow and children of the late Mr Henry Bates. The Rev. R Tuson was chairman with a number of pianists and vocalists performing, then the report states: "The meeting also had the pleasure of hearing and seeing the author of 'Oakey's Keeker', Mr T. Armstrong and as might be expected, he was well received." Sadly, Henry Bates, a joiner by trade, had died at Collierly in December 1877 at the age of thirty eight[7].

The local newspaper in 1880, reported on a 'Benefit Concert at Tantobie' on behalf of Mr John Evans who had been laid up many weeks by an accident[8]. The report told of various performances by artistes then said, "To crown all, there was the local poetry manufactured on the spot by Mr T. Armstrong, the Tanfield Poet, who added fresh laurels to his already high reputation as a rhymer by his achievements in that line on Saturday evening."

Mr John Thomas Robinson, a resident of Tanfield Lea kept a diary from 1891 to 1902 which is held at Beamish Regional Resource Centre. An entry dated Saturday 20th June 1896 refers to Tommy and his brother Henry Armstrong calling to seek subscriptions to 'Dr. James Ward's Testimonial Fund'. This shows that as well as performing in concerts, Tommy was willing to go from door to door to collect for charitable purposes.

In 1901, the local newspaper reported on a 'Magic Lantern and Gramophone Entertainment' in the Primitive Methodist Church, Tanfield Lea in aid of the new Sunday School Fund[9]. Tommy had charge of the gramophone and gave songs and selections at intervals. Earlier that year, reference had been made in the newspaper[10] to Tommy's love of his gramophone – the column 'WE KNOW' read: "That the Tanfield Poet and 'Cross-Bar' have at length made each other's acquaintance. That Tommy loves his gramophone almost as much as one of the ladies from the brick flats." Cross-Bar was the writer of the newspaper column 'Football Notes and News' and the comment about one of the ladies from the brick flats, refers to the occasion when Tommy appeared before 'Tanfield School Board' as explained earlier in this book.

In addition to these specific events, other reports talk in general about him giving his services for the benefit of others. Such an example is in the Editor's footnote to a letter published in the local newspaper in 1916[11]. The relevant part reads: "Tommy did much in his time to lighten the cares of the people by his amusing songs and he gave services at entertainments time out of number, readily and free for the benefit of others."

In 1951, WHA spoke well of his father Tommy by saying, "No man did more in raising money for needy cases sixty years ago"[12].

Anne Armstrong and her grandfather John Willie Armstrong who knew Tommy well, are both mentioned in more detail in Chapter 6. John Willie told Anne that there were numerous occasions when Tommy would stand at the entrance to the pit with his cap in his hand, making a collection for an injured miner or a bereaved family. He made similar collections in the Working Men's Club. The miners all knew Tommy, appreciated what he was doing and realised that his next collection could be on behalf of them or their families. As a result, no one refused to contribute when Tommy was making a collection. This is another good example of how Tommy always wanted to help others in any way he could.

Collecting for injured miners and their families.

Chapter 3
MOVE TO WHITLEY BAY

In February 1902, the local newspaper told its readers that Tommy was shortly to move to Whitley Bay to start business as a Newsagent[1]. In March, the newspaper confirmed he had made the move and started the business, and "That Tommy had a windfall recently. Lucky fellah."[2]

In May the same year, the newspaper published the following satirical letter that Tommy sent from Whitley Bay[3] about a racehorse named 'Checkweigher'. A Checkweigher was a mine owner's representative, who checked on the weight and quality of coal coming up from the mine in tubs and Checkweighers were generally unpopular with the mine workers.

The letter refers to Tommy giving the horse a rubbing with 'Pro-Boer Mixture'. The term 'Pro-Boer' at that time, was the misleading name given to those who opposed the Government's policy of fighting in the Boer War of 1899 to 1902[4]. The letter also refers to Tommy giving the horse a pint of 'Gregory's Mixture'. In the Victorian era, this was a stimulant and laxative consisting of two parts rhubarb, four parts calcined magnesia and one part ginger[5]. It is not surprising that the horse galloped well after these two applications by Tommy.

TANFIELD POET – WHITLEY NEWSAGENT

Dear Sir – Please oblige your old friend Tommy with a small space in your valuable newspaper. In the first place, I send my best respects to all my old neighbours and acquaintances. They won't know me when they come down to Whitley. I am getting so stout I cannot stoop to fasten my boots. I blame my weight and my horse not being fit for running in the West Stanley Stakes, for losing this great event, but if my horse-club manager and Tommy the Poet be spared until the next big race, there will be great odds on, because the people in West Stanley know that he can run and they likewise know that my experience as a jockey cannot be excelled. I knew my horse was not fit for running that day but I knew there was a great deal of public money on him. I would advise the people in Stanley to save their money until the next race. There will be ten to one on Club Manager and Tommy the Poet.

I have only had two mounts this season. I have rode a winner and a loser. I have made a mistake in saying I rode a winner. I rode him in his trial gallop but not for the stakes. The people of Tanfield sent their horse, Checkweigher, down to Whitley to be trained by Tommy the Poet. I have seen this horse run many a time in the County of Durham and I cannot remember of him being defeated, therefore I had every confidence in him for this race. My confidence increased when we got on to Whitley Links on the following day after his arrival. I just gave him a gentle canter as far as St Mary's Island and back the first day to

St Mary's Island, Whitley Bay.

show him the ground before preparing him for his final gallop. He lost a shoe off beside the Whitley Convalescent Home. Tom Temple of Shield Row brought it to the stable; him and me took Checkweigher to get shod. He was so fresh he would not stand, so we were compelled to lay him on his back and sit on his belly to keep him down. Checkweigher is the only horse I have seen shod upside down. The blacksmith says he was the smartest horse that he ever had in his shop.

We then took him back to the stable and I gave him a good feed of county average and a drink of overweight which he seemed to enjoy. I then took off my coat and gave him a good rubbing with Pro-Boer Mixture, but he did not care for it; he commenced to kick and I was forced to leave him alone. After a night's rest, I went to the stable in the morning and found him full of life. I gave him a pint of Gregory's Mixture and prepared him for a two mile gallop, which he finished up in grand style without a turned hair on him. It was the quickest ride I have had since Corry's Rat flew from Tanfield.

But I will conclude for the present, wishing Checkweigher and his jockey every success in all their future events – be sure and give my best respects to Jimmy Robinson and yourself.

> If you should come down here to stop,
> And you should want a shave or crop;
> Be sure and call at Tommy's shop,
> I've got a champion barber.
> In summer time I've rooms to let,
> Where every comfort you can get;
> I keep cigars and cigarettes,
> Call when you come to Whitley.

> TOMMY ARMSTRONG

In September the same year, the newspaper[6] reminded its readers that Tommy had 'flitted away to Whitley Bay' and related parts of a couple of his poems. It also included:-

"Tommy, as we have already said, is now living at Whitley Bay, where he is engaged in literary pursuits. Besides writing and selling his own poetry, he supplies the entire district with daily, weekly and periodical literature. All his old friends and they are legion, will be delighted to hear that he is succeeding famously."

In spite of considerable research of newspapers local to Whitley Bay, Electoral Registers, Directories and other records, no address can be linked to Tommy with any certainty. It is not known exactly when he returned to North West Durham but the next evidence that he was there, was when he registered the death of his fifteen year old daughter Barbara Alice Armstrong in June 1906 when he showed his address as Chapel Row, Ouston. Tommy then remained in the area until he died at Tantobie in 1920.

Centre of Whitley Bay circa 1910.

Chapter 4
AILING HEALTH AND HIS DEATH

Numerous references have been made to Tommy suffering from strokes. In poems and letters to newspapers, he himself refers to strokes as 'afflictions'.

His first stroke was probably in 1899 when he was aged only fifty and he spent some time in 'Whitley Home'. This was the Prudhoe Memorial Convalescent Home at Whitley Links, Whitley Bay which opened in 1869, closed in 1959 and was later demolished. The Home was named after Algernon Percy, 4th Duke of Northumberland, formerly Lord Prudhoe. A Leisure Pool which opened in 1974 now stands on the site. In 1899, the local newspaper published the following letter which Tommy wrote from the Home[1]:

THE TANFIELD POET

Sir, – Will you kindly allow me a little space in your valuable columns in which to thank the workmen of Tanfield Lea Colliery for their kindness towards me and my family during my affliction. As I am not able to express my thankfulness in a perfect way, I shall content myself with thanking the four men who gave themselves the trouble to arrange a subscription and also each subscriber. May each one at present in good health remain so in future. I have always done my best to help to raise and cheer the heart of the widow and succour the fatherless and I am no worse today for what I have done, and if health permit, I shall be glad at any time to assist a lame dog over a stile. With sincere thanks and best wishes to all.

THOMAS ARMSTRONG
Whitley Home

Tommy obviously continued to suffer because when the 1911 Census was taken, he was living with his widowed daughter Mary Robson and her nine children and he was shown as an 'Invalid'. Tommy suffered again in 1913 and in March that year he wrote the following letter to the local newspaper[2]:

TOMMY ARMSTRONG, PITMAN'S POET

Sir, – Will you oblige me by inserting these few lines in your valuable paper? I know it is my duty to return thanks to three young men in Tanfield Lea. Their names are as follows:- John Milburn, James Street; John Burrell, John Street and Thomas Christopher, Allan Square. I

Published by B. Graham, Whitley Bay.

Prudhoe Memorial Convalescent Home, Whitley Links, Whitley Bay.

cannot find words to express my thankfulness for the kind act they have done for me by raising a public subscription. I return my sincere thanks to those three young men, likewise to every subscriber and hope their future prospect is and will be much better than mine. It was always my ambition to help a lame or afflicted person, male or female. I feel proud when I think of the good that I did when I was able to do it. I am as willing to-day as I was then, but I am not as able; but I will conclude for the present. All being well, I will interest you next week. I will tell you about being at an Oxo social.

TOMMY ARMSTRONG
Pitman's Poet

In April that same year, a grand benefit concert was given at The Star Cinema, Tantobie in aid of Tommy. It was reported that "Special turns were engaged for the night and we were glad to see the public turn up in large numbers to patronise the popular poet."[3]

Tommy continued to suffer and in 1914, another concert was held for his benefit, this time at the Club Hall, Tantobie which was crowded. The newspaper report refers to Tommy having composed over 150 poems and arranged no fewer than 85 benefit concerts in the area. It also states that Tommy 'suffered a stroke about five years ago and has been unable to follow his employment since.'[4]

NOTE: This is particularly interesting because in recent years, many people have wondered why no poem can be found that was written by Tommy about the terrible disaster at West Stanley Colliery in February 1909, when 168 men and boys were killed. It was thought that as for most disasters in the area, Tommy must have written a poem but it was one of those which have been lost forever. Five years before this concert in 1914 it was 1909 when he would have had the stroke referred to. It is therefore most likely that ill health prevented Tommy from writing at the time of the West Stanley disaster which could explain the absence of a poem by him about the tragedy.

In 1916, the local newspaper published a letter from a reader, at the end of which was the following footnote from the Editor of the newspaper[5]:-

"We wish to add to our contributor's articles by drawing attention to Mr Armstrong's present needy condition. An effort is, we believe being made locally to raise some financial assistance and we hope that there will be a generous response. 'Tommy' did much in his time to lighten the cares of the people by his amusing songs and he gave services at entertainment times out of number, readily and free for the benefit of others. The time has come when practical acknowledgement is needed to ease the struggle of declining health and advancing years. He has a brother, Mr Henry Armstrong, who lives in one of the Tanfield Lea Miners' Homes. – Ed."

A few days after his last stroke, Tommy died of apoplexy on the 30th August 1920 at 2 Havelock Terrace, Tantobie. He was buried at Tanfield St Margaret Church Yard on the 2nd September 1920 in the presence of a large assembly of people. The Rev. F Pickering, Superintendent Minister of the Stanley Primitive Methodist Circuit conducted the burial service. On the same day that he was buried, the *Stanley News* carried a tribute:

"The death of "Tommy" Armstrong, after much suffering in his declining years, removes a popular local figure, one who has perhaps created more fun for his fellow residents in North West Durham than any other man. "Tommy" had a genius for humour. It bubbled from his lips under all circumstances, a constant flow of genuine mirth and wit. The trials of his later years and his continued ill-health would have altered many men but "Tommy" remained ever happy and hopeful through all his ills."

At the time of his burial, there was no memorial headstone for his grave but a letter to the newspaper in February 1924 suggested it would be fitting to have one erected [6]. As a result, a Committee was formed under the Chairmanship of Joshua Charlton (Chairman of Tanfield Urban Council), with Robert Bell as Secretary, Mr P. Duffy, JP as

Treasurer and a number of other local dignitaries as committee members. A successful public subscription was arranged and in June that year, the Committee Secretary (Robert Bell) wrote a letter to the newspaper which was published thanking everyone who had subscribed to 'The Tommy Armstrong Memorial Fund'[7]. The headstone was erected soon afterwards[8].

Headstone from Tommy's grave.

Chapter 5
NEWSPAPER CORRESPONDENT

In addition to the letters referred to elsewhere in this book, Tommy wrote other letters to newspapers. They were very funny and written in dialect, so they may be a little tricky for those to read who are not familiar with 'pitmatic' but they are worth persevering with. The letters are set out below.

The Consett Chronicle - 14th September 1900.

THE TANFIELD POETS BIRTHDAY

Mr Editor – Aw naw yil be offended it me for not retein befor noo but aw naw yil think nowt eboot it wen aw tell ye hoo au've been situated lately. Aw ad eboot two thoosind visitors it wor hoose on the fifteenth iv last munth. Yil mebbie think aw's tellen e lee, but au'l tell ye the reason aw ad see mony visitors. It wis maw borth day. Yis, aw wis two pund twelve (aw meen fifty-two) the fifteenth iv last munth. Aw wis born it Shotley Bridge, in Wood Street, on th' fifteenth dae iv Augist, hiteteen hundred en forty hite, en its twenty yeer since aw ad e borth dae befor, so aw thowt aw wid injoi mesel for feer aw ad nee mair.

Ye may depend thare wis e demonstoraishon here. Th' pits eboots there stopt drawn coals it fowor ec'lock it eftorneun. Th' cocoa nuts wis fleeing it Stanley, th' shuggy boats wis on full swing, en thare wis sum soop consumed it Airmstrang's cook shop, en it il tuaik me enuthur fortnith te get things put reet. En then aw's gan te hev e trip te see maw borth place once mor. Its thorty-two yeer since aw wis it Shotley, en aw dinet expect te see mony aw ken wen aw dee gan. Aw nivor did naw monny at Shotley. Aw wis only yung wen aw com in tid, en aw wis only yung wen aw com oot on't. But aw kin remember iv e canny awd wumin th' cauld Betty Redshaw, but she'l not be thare noo. Poor awd sowl, she was the forst womin thit weshd en drest th' Tanfield Poet. En hoo paishint she was.

Aw wasint vary gud te deel with it th' time, becaws aw wis e vary big boy wen aw wis vary little. But th' langer aw lived, th' better we get acquented. Mr Editor, aw wid like te heh yor company wen aw gan te see Wood Street, but if ye shud be doon befor aw gan ye mite tell thim thit tharel be a stranger caulen sum dae befor lang. Ye cin tell them e greet stoot chap, with big black beerd en rings on awl hees fingers but hite, en buaith hands in his pockets, but nowt else. Still aw think aw bettor send thim word me sel, en give thim time te get things ridy for decoraiten th' street. Thor shure tee de that, wen they naw thit e Prime Ministor, born it Shotley Bridge, wis gan te pay them e visit. Then eftor we lunch we Mistor Preestmins en uthors, we'l hav a luk throo the Papor Mill ther, ware maw muthor yuse te work; en, if its e fine dae, we'l hev a luk once more it th' Spa Grunds, ware au've sat en drank

monny e pot e tee, en injoid me sel we th' taisty bites provided for th'
Sundae Skeul bairns it time on the Band of Hope dae. Ye could see
hundreds e Sunday Skeul scholars we pots tied up in a white
hankutchor. It wis we te heh th' bonniest pot. Teachors freh each skeul
wis thare te luk eftor thor awn scholars.

Then te muaik th' dae bettor, we ad it wor heed th' Shotley Drum en
Fife Band. It wis th' crack e th' dae it that time. Aw wis only yung
then, but aw've hard nowt tee beet thim since, en that's forty-five years
ago. Aw's nee judge e musick, but aw judge thor instramints. Aw naw
the difforance between e fife en e cornit, but aw bettor conclude for th'
present. Th' callor il be cumen just noo. Tell Elizah Dubs aw wis
asking eftor hor. Aw want e housekeeper. Aw'l mebbie see her wen aw
cum te caul ipon ye te gan we me te Shotley. Wait we paishons.
Awl'rite e bit oftinor noo. Aw'l try te send sumthing ivory week.

TOMMY AIRMSTRANG
TANFIELD POET

Shotley Bridge Paper Mill where Tommy's mother worked.

The Stanley News and North West Durham Observer - 7th November 1913.

CLOU DEEN WEDDIN

Mistor Editor – Aw wis vary much disepointed last week-end. Aw bilt
mesel up on ganin te Sunderland te see th' football match; but aw
did'nt get. But divvent think it wis for th' want e munny. Wei no! Aw

had fowerpince-ha'pney nivvor brockin inte. Auve been suaiven up for six weeks. It's istonishen wat munny ye can suaive iv e short time. But Aul tell ye wat stopt me fra getten te th' football match. Aw gat en invitashon tiv e weddin'. So Aw thowt Aw wid gan thare. Aw fadint be se sair crusht; but wen Aw gat there, Aw cud 'ardly get in. Thare wis vary neer is mony thare is ther waus at th' football

Clough Dene.

match, en such e set oot es Aw nivor saw befor'. Th' weddin' wis celebraited en carried oot at Cloe' Deen, et th' hoose iv Mistor en Misteris Musgrove, th' parints e th' bride. Th' bride wis Miss Mary Musgrove, en th' bridegroom wis Maister Frederick Oyston, of Logan Hoose. He is th' grandson of aud Joe Oyston, e man thit is respectid be everybody thit kens 'im, en so is awl th' fam'ly.

> Te speek of th' bride's fathor, likewise th' bride's muthor.
> Aw nue them buaith befor' thae nue eech uthor.
> Aw wis plees'd for te see th' changes since then,
> Thae hev e nice family, buaith wimmin en men;
> In e yem e thor awn ther livin' content,
> Thare's neebody gans tea ax thim for rent:
> Fer by this grand cottage thare's a greet lump e grund,
> Te grow thor awn stuff, which suaives mony e pund.
> Th' sons en th' dowtors aul works hand en hand,
> En lucks eftor yem comforts, en likewise the land:
> If ye gan be Tantoby, ye gan throo Clou' Deen,
> It's th' forst thit ye cum tee, it's plane te be seen,
> Ware this happy family in comfort reside,
> Wauken or riding', it's on th' reet side.

Mistor Editor, – Eftor we had e gud feed en e grand eftorneun's intortanemint, we muaid wor wae te' Tantoby Stor' Haul. It wis ingaig'd tiv elivin that neet. En mind, we 'ad e jolly time on't. Miss Yewison wis at th' peeano, en she wis kept ganen aul neet. En believe me, she can plae. Th' bride's unkil Jack Boril, en me danst tiv aw wis forst te sit doon. Buaith mei legs es bent ivor since; but aw's glad Jack's nee warse. Ivoryone thit wis thare wis ment for injoymint, en thor waus sum. Thor nivor wis e rang word menshin'd. It elivin e' clock we muaid off te wor yems. That finished th' Setorda's fun, Mistor Editor: Aw wis quite setesfied we th' Setorda, but Aw 'ad te gan back th' next dae, Sunda'. Ye wud wundor ware aul th' foaks cum freh. Eftor we 'ad oor tees, Aw wis invited inte th' parlour end te see th' prisints th' bride en bridegroom 'ad getten. Th' room wis packt we soft waire en 'ard waire. Thare wis ivorything Aw kin menshin, but a motor car. So aw bid them aul gud neet, en went off yem.

> May the bride and bridegroom live a long and healthful life,
> For other eighty year to come may they be man and wife;
> And may their friends on either side be sociable and agree,
> And should a Fred or Mary come, to them be kind and free.

TOMMY AIRMSTRANG,
Pitman Poet, Tantoby

NOTE: There actually was a marriage at that time between Frederick L. Oyston and Eleanor Mary Musgrove and it may well be that Tommy attended the wedding.

The Consett and Stanley Chronicle – 2nd March 1917.

TOMMY THE POET'S LETTER

Mister Editor – Th last lettor aw rote aw menshind what changes thair'd been since ye en me met, en thairs been sum mair since then. Its nearly twelve months since Look Recen, Ned Inglish en me wis examined it Stanla be th military doctors en the sade then thit we needint fret. Thae sade my failing was, aw only had one lung, en Ned's failing was he ad e impeedemint iv hees speech, en Look lost th last battil he fit. Wadint ye wunder hoo thae get ten naw these things, Mistor Editor, aw naw yil ardly believe me wen aw tell ye wat thiv deun, but its troo.

We've aul three gettin war paipors te be it Nuecassil te meet th military authoritys on the twenty second dae of February. Isint that clever. Eftor tellin es thit we wid nivor pass. Wor ald willing eneuf te gan, it wer forad, but aws not very much sorprised when aw think eboot wats cumen. Its th big push cumen on, en thae want aul thor best men for te finish the war. Th Kaisor en Hinderbarg il both get thor watchis brokin this time, but if thae ad letting us gan when we wantid te gan, things wid e been different noo, but aw hoap thairl be nee mair wars eftor this ones owor. The War loans awl reet, aw wish thaird been e war loan wen aw wis a lad, en putin a penny a week in thid ivor since aw cud ebowt e nue fut en duen ewae we bessy, but awl se hoo aw gan on. Awve putin a penny e week in te the war loan ivor since it started, awl hev e gud draw it th finish, Mistor Editor.

Aws raithor disepointed th forst fine dae we get aw did intend te hev e ride doon te Shotily Bridge. It wis th forst plaice thait aw livd in wen aw caw te th Coonty e Durhom, sixty hite eers since. Me faithor en muthor en me com frea Cairlile in Cumborlind, but aw nue vary little eboot Cumborlind wen we left. But aw ken e bit eboot Shotily Bridge, en aw've a gud reet. Au wis born thare on th fifteenth iv August. Aw warnd we adint a golly time ont. Aw wis surprised te see eis many wumin foaks sitten be th fire side en bed side. It must heh been tauk't eboot emang thim aboot me cumin. Aw adint been lang emang thim tiv aw ard aud Betty Ridshaw sae te me muthor aw think awl wesh hm en we me beein e straingor aw thowt sh sade thresh him; aw teuk hor up rang. If Betty ad putten e finger on me aw wid e gon bac te Cumborlind, but aw got e gud wesh en aw wis drest up te th mark. Wen aw sor aw was welcum aw muaid me mind up te stop, so if aw cin catch e fine dae awl hev e ride te Shotily te hev e luck it number siventeen, th cottage ware Tommy wis born, if aw divint gan te France.

> I was born at Shotley Bridge I've heard my mother say;
> 'Twas in the month of August, and on the fifteenth day;
> There was plenty ginger beer, and whips of Stewart's tea;
> I looked for something stronger, but there was none to see.
>
> That is why I never take strong drink at night or morn
> I take what other people took that morning I was born.
> I may come in a motor car, or I may come on a flat;
> You will know me when I come by my round square hat.

TOMMY ARMSTRONG
(Pitman Poet)
Tanfield Lea

The Stanley News Office.

Chapter 6
THE CHARACTER AND ALLEGED DRUNKARD

Ivan Garnham, a retired Headmaster of Tanfield Lea Junior School, gives a fine example of the humour of Tommy. Ivan's father told him of an occasion when Tommy who was bow legged, met another miner in the street who was knock kneed. Tommy suggested that they swap trousers as it might straighten their legs, thereby doing them both a favour.

In 1951, Tommy's son WHA made the following comments about his father[1]:
i) He was a champion quoits player in his day – ten yards on the clay, but he was also a champion drinker which kept him and his family down.
ii) Drink was his downfall.

In 1952, WHA went on to make the following additional comments about Tommy[2]:
i) Me dad's muse was a mug of beer.
ii) The effect which beer has on a genius is remarkable. My father always wrote his best songs when he had had one over the eight. Whiskey would not have had the same effect on him.
iii)He had an indomitable thirst. He got songs printed on broadsides which he sold round the pubs, a penny a time, to raise beer money.

It is worthy of mention at this point, that prior to the above comments being made public by WHA, no such comments can be attributed to anyone else before that time; not Tommy's close brother Henry nor anyone else who contributed to newspaper articles. Since 1951, authors and narrators have been only too pleased to repeat and in some cases exaggerate the extent of Tommy's alleged drinking habits – it makes for a better story.

The Oak Tree Inn, Tantobie – one of Tommy's local pubs.

40

Certainly, WHA influenced the minds of residents in the village of Tanfield Lea by accusing Tommy of excessive drinking. In February 2007, *Inside Out* – a television programme on BBC1 North – featured three items, one of which was about Tommy and a few people contributed to the commentary. Whilst some of the programme was very complimentary about Tommy's prowess as a poet, there were a few comments which were derogatory about him as a person, such as:

"For decades after his death, he was disowned by residents of Tanfield Lea."

"Residents did not like being reminded he had been one of their community."

"Drink confined him to poverty."

"Residents did not want to talk about Tommy who was a disgrace and closed their doors in the faces of callers."

"Residents were good Methodist people who were against drinking."

Unfortunately, the television programme does not indicate when the commentators met with these experiences but if it was shortly before the programme was made in 2007, it is unlikely that many, if any residents were old enough to have remembered Tommy who died in 1920. The likelihood is that they were making such comments based on what had originated from WHA who was an influential figure in the village.

An example of how WHA tried to influence others about Tommy comes from Gerald Ash who was raised in Tanfield Lea. Gerald was one of the Cadets of the Sons of Temperance Society which was run by WHA and he recalls that at a meeting about 1947, he asked WHA to tell them about his father. WHA responded by saying his father's name was not to be mentioned and intimated that he was a drunkard. The chances are that WHA influenced others with his views and they in turn passed on that opinion as if it was fact.

Anne Armstrong and her grandfather John William Armstrong (1896-1988)

Anne is a descendant of Tommy's close brother Henry and she still lives in the North West area of County Durham. Her grandfather, known as John Willie, was twenty four when Tommy died and knew him well. Anne and John Willie spent a lot of time together and he was pleased to answer Anne's questions about family members. Some interesting and relevant information about Tommy comes from John Willie via Anne. During his latter years, Tommy lived at Tantobie with John Willie's parents, Timothy & Amelia Armstrong who helped to look after him when he was ill. Whilst this was the 'done thing', they were very fond of Tommy who always appreciated what they and others did for him.

As a youngster, John Willie remembered Tommy as a 'funny man' who amused the children. As well as the funny poems which made them laugh, Tommy liked to play practical jokes and tease them which often exasperated the adults.

For many years, Timothy Armstrong and his Uncle Tommy lived and worked either together or near each other. They were both members of Tantobie Working Men's Club which, as he got older, was Tommy's favourite 'watering hole' where he knew everyone, was related to many and was guaranteed to provide entertainment. Tommy gathered a lot of material for his poems from the club but also at John Willie's home, where he sat for hours talking with several callers about the pit and personalities.

John Willie disputed the claim that Tommy sold printed copies of his works for beer money but was certainly aware that they were sold to raise money for worthy causes in the area. Tommy, as well as many other miners, enjoyed his beer but no one could be described as an alcoholic. Those who drank did so because they liked to and stopped when the money was gone. Tommy was fortunate in that he frequently had drinks bought for him in the pub or club by an audience who were appreciative of the entertainment he gave them. Wives and families of the drinking men inevitably suffered neglect to some extent but they did not suffer from 'want'. In those days, 'want' implied that the workhouse was looming and if Tommy did not 'have a penny to his name', then neither did most of those around him.

John Willie remembered that Tommy's favourite meal of the day was his breakfast of bacon and cheese baked in the oven. He would later set off up to the Club and he caused much humour at the time with his habit of refusing lifts in horses and traps from well meaning passers-by. "I'll get there quicker walking," would be his retort.

Anne once asked her grandfather how he remembered Tommy, "As an Uncle, a Poet, a Drinker, a Unionist or a Pitman?" John Willie replied, "Tommy was a little fellow with a good heart who made a bit of difference in the lives of the folk he knew."

In 1863, Robert Wilson MD published a paper entitled 'The Coal Miners of Durham and Northumberland: their Habits and Diseases'[3]. As a Doctor who for many years, attended daily to the ailments of pitmen, he knew about their lifestyle and was well qualified to write about it. A relevant part of his paper reads:

"Great excesses are still prevalent on the pay Friday and Saturday nights. Ale is the liquor chiefly drunk. But no matter what excesses a man may commit on the pay weekend, he must be at his post on the Monday following, or run the risk of being discharged; so that the habitual drunkard is sure to lose his employment. In all my experience among them I have never known a case of dipsomania, nor have I had to treat a single case of delirium tremens: this is more than I can say for many other callings."

This supports the information and views passed down by John Willie Armstrong.

Amongst the mining community, there were two camps of miners, those who liked a drink and those who followed the church. Tommy and WHA were in opposite camps but why, in the later stages of WHA's life, he chose to castigate his father will never be fully known. Tommy fathered and provided for fourteen children, albeit only six survived to adult age but there is no evidence of any of the other five turning against their father as WHA did. As has been shown earlier, Tommy was willing to provide his services for charitable purposes at venues other than public houses, including Woodside Primitive Methodist Church, which was the Church with which WHA was deeply involved. He was obviously a good man with no ill feeling towards his fellow men. WHA on the other hand, if he was not always that way inclined, became intolerant towards anyone, including his father, who drank any alcohol at all.

That said, WHA was only too pleased to publish a 'Song Book' containing 25 of Tommy's works and to claim proprietorship of them. The first edition, presumably prepared in collaboration with Tommy who signed underneath his photograph in the book, was published in 1909 (eleven years before Tommy's death) and sold at three pence. The second edition, published in 1930 (ten years after Tommy's death) was a repeat of the same 25 works and sold at three pence. In the Preface to this edition, WHA included, "I am busy preparing all his compositions for a final book to be issued at an early date which I hope will meet the wishes of the public." Twenty two years later, WHA presumably thought it was time he did something about publishing the 'final book' because on the 23rd October 1952, the front page of the *Stanley News* made an appeal on his behalf: "For the co-operation of our readers in loaning him anything that was composed by his father apart from the 25 songs that are already in print". The newspaper said WHA wanted these because he was busy collecting material for the life story of Tommy. However, WHA died ten months later without publishing anything further. After he died in 1953, friends of his published a third edition of the original book which sold for one shilling.

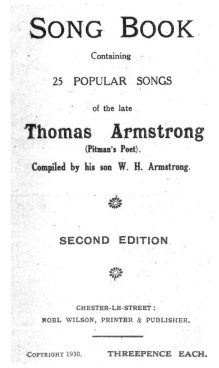

SONG BOOK

Containing

25 POPULAR SONGS

of the late

Thomas Armstrong
(Pitman's Poet).

Compiled by his son W. H. Armstrong.

❀

SECOND EDITION

❀

CHESTER-LE-STREET :
NOEL WILSON, PRINTER & PUBLISHER.

COPYRIGHT 1930.   THREEPENCE EACH.

Front Cover of the Second Edition of the 'Song Book' of Tommy's works.

It seems odd that WHA castigated his father but was happy to 'ride on the back' of his success, even to the extent of wishing to write the life story of Tommy. It is sad that WHA portrayed Tommy as a 'drunkard' when evidence indicates, yes, he liked a drink but certainly could not be described as a 'drunkard'.

Chapter 7
CONTROVERSIES

In 1916, the local newspaper published a letter from an acquaintance who had known Tommy all his life[1]. Part of the letter gives the following interesting account of one of Tommy's experiences:

"Tommy had some strange experiences during his poetic career. In 1866 he was apprehended at the Addison Colliery near Blaydon. Three Police Officers took him out of bed. You will wonder why? Tommy had written some poetry for funeral cards and a travelling Jew was to frame these cards and print them for a certain sum but on delivering the goods he charged a brother of Tommy's two shillings more than agreed upon. This raised Tommy's anger and when the Jew came round again, he made the old man believe he was going to kill him, locking the door. The old man was seriously alarmed and when liberated went and took out a warrant for his apprehension for threatening to kill him and on the 6th day of August three policemen came to take Tommy to Blaydon Police Station where he was in custody for three days. He suffered no further but for all his intended fun he never got his money back from the Jew, the only man that ever took him down. He made a few verses on this episode."

No record of this event can be found in local newspapers, probably because Tommy never appeared at Court. The story is probably correct

STELLA COLLIERY. 1159.

Stella Colliery which was also known as Addison Colliery owned by Stella Co.

because Tommy and his close brother Henry were both still alive in 1916 and were themselves communicating with the local newspaper at that time. If the story had not been true, either Tommy or Henry would undoubtedly have written in to contradict it but no letters from them appeared in subsequent newspapers. At the time of this event in 1866, Tommy and his older brother William were both working as hewers in the Brockwell Seam at Addison Colliery[2] so it was probably William who was charged the extra two shillings by the Jew. Also, even though there is not a Police Station at Blaydon nowadays, there was one there in 1866[3].

That same letter to the newspaper in 1916 referred to another occasion when Joseph Elliott, the Keeker at Oakey's Colliery went to Lanchester Petty Sessions to complain about Tommy. The following funny report of this event was published in an earlier local newspaper in 1878[4]:

ALLEGED LIBEL ON A "KEEKER" AT SHIELD ROW

Yesterday (Thursday) afternoon after the ordinary police business at Lanchester Petty Sessions had been disposed of, Mr Joseph Elliott, a "Keeker" at Oakey's Colliery appeared before the Magistrates (Messrs. Kearney and Clavering) and asked their advice under the following circumstances. A local comic song book had been published by a person named "Tommy Armstrong, Oakey's Poet," in which certain reflections were made on the applicant. He wanted to know if he could prosecute the writer for "libel and scandal."
The Chairman (Mr Kearney), looking at the objectionable song said he observed the writer called Mr Elliott a "hairy faced rascal."
The Clerk (Mr Watson): What particular portion of the song do you consider libellous?

Mr Elliott having marked the song at a particular spot, the Chairman read as follows:-

> Now, Joey Elliott, you silly old man!
> You have nearly done all the ill you can;
> With age your whiskers are turning grey,
> I think it is time you were starting to pray.
> I never did like to wish anyone harm;
> But I doubt you will go to a place where it's warm;
> It's nothing but right to reap what you sow –
> They'll burn your whiskers, Old Maiden Law Joe!

The Clerk: Are you any worse for this?
Mr Elliott: I am not any better. I cannot walk about.
The Clerk: You are no worse for being called "hairy faced." You still have your whiskers. (Laughter) You will not be injured by the song unless you lose your situation or your standing in society.
Mr Elliott: I cannot pass along the highway without people firing shots at me.
The Clerk: If people fire shots at you and injure you, you can bring

them up for unlawfully wounding you. (Laughter)

Mr Elliott: But it is not my body the shots hurt. It is my feelings. (Renewed laughter)

The Clerk: Oh, it's your feelings is it? If the Magistrates think you have been libelled you may bring the person here and the Justices may commit him to the Assizes. In a criminal prosecution for libel you would have to pay the costs. You might bring a civil action against him however and then you could claim damages. I cannot say what damages the jury would award but they might give you a farthing. (Laughter)

The Chairman: Why are you called "Maiden Law Joe?"

Mr Elliott: I cannot say.

The Clerk: I see the poet calls you a "cruel imposter." Is that part of what you complain about?

Mr Elliott: I did not come here to contend with the Magistrates. I came here to seek their advice.

The Clerk: You have not had your wages decreased since the song was published, have you? (Laughter)

Mr Elliott: I did not come here to be made a fool of. (Renewed laughter) I came here to ask advice in a civilised court but it appears to me –

The Clerk: If you have a complaint to make, you will have to lay an Information.

Mr Elliott: I have done so.

The Clerk: But you will have to make it in writing. You had better consult your solicitor.

Mr Elliott: I expected to see Mr Granger but as he is not here, I thought it was my duty to come before the Magistrates. I am entitled to the law of the land as well as any other person. I wish to know if this case could be disposed of here, or should it come before a superior court?

The Clerk: The Magistrates could deal with it in the way I have told you.

The Chairman: I advise you to let the matter alone.

Mr Elliott: I did not think I could come to a better place than this for advice. At the same time I ought to have civil advice.

The Clerk: You have got it and for nothing.

The Chairman: Mr Watson has said nothing uncivil to you.

Mr Elliott: (Preparing to take his leave) I think he has behaved to me very indifferently. (Laughter) Mr Watson ought not to laugh at me.

The Chairman: One cannot help laughing as the thing is so very funny.

Mr Elliott: It has done me no harm but at the same time, I don't like it to be sung in the streets of Newcastle and handed down from one generation to another. (Laughter)

The Chairman: It will immortalise you. (More laughter)

Mr Elliott: This is the first time I have come before you and I am very sorry. I am very much offended to come here and be laughed at. (Mr Elliott then folded up the song book and left the Court, evidently much displeased).

These stories have been published in various places since the letter to the newspaper in 1916 but often vary from the factual reports shown above.

THE ALLEGED THIEF

No one could be criticised for believing that Tommy was sentenced to six months imprisonment in Durham Jail for stealing a pair of pit stockings from the Co-operative Store at West Stanley. Enough reports of the 'story' have been published in books, on internet web-sites and on DVDs as if it is a definite fact.

Sadly, we again find that Tommy's son WHA was the originator of this 'story'. In 1951, when referring to Tommy writing 'Trimdon Grange Explosion' in 1882, WHA said, "Shortly after this, he and another chap were sent to Durham Gaol for supposed stealing; they got the sentence of six months and while in gaol he composed the song 'Durham Gaol' to the tune 'Nee gud luck aboot th' Hoose'. He wrote it on the back of the door and when seen by the authorities, he was released."[5] WHA repeated the story in 1952 but omitted any reference to the second man he had mentioned the previous year[6].

Since then, the 'story' has been published many times and to make it sound better, some authors have exaggerated it to say Tommy was drunk at the time and he was tempted by a pair of pit stockings on display in West Stanley Co-op. They were the only pair of bow legged ones he had seen and being small and bow legged himself, he thought they would be ideal for him. The second man referred to by WHA in 1951, has never featured in any of the published versions of the 'story'.

Considerable research has been undertaken but no trace can be

Durham Gaol.

found of any references to this 'story' in any local newspapers, particularly in the years 1882/83 which is when WHA claims the supposed theft took place. Unfortunately, no records of prisoners in Durham Jail have survived prior to 1902 and no records prior to 1915 have survived for Lanchester Petty Sessions, which is where Tommy would have appeared. All other available records have been researched – Quarter Sessions, Police (Public Access Office under the Freedom of Information Act), The National Archives and Durham County Record Office but Tommy does not feature anywhere for this alleged offence.

Earlier in this chapter, there are details of two police/court related matters which were told by a man in 1916 who had known Tommy all his life. Having related those two events, it is unlikely he would have omitted reference to the alleged theft by Tommy, had it been true.

In recent times, it has been suggested that by virtue of the content of the poem 'Durham Gaol', Tommy must have been a prisoner there to learn about what he wrote in the poem. The poem has been analysed in great detail and most, if not all of the content, would have been common knowledge. Any of the content thought not to be common knowledge, could easily have been learnt by Tommy from fellow miners who had been inmates at the gaol. At the time of the 1881 Census, out of 411 male prisoners in Durham Gaol, 63 were coal miners and more would have been coming and going throughout the years, with every likelihood of some being known by Tommy.

The story, initiated by WHA, was first published in 1952[7] and subsequent authors of the story may have accepted it without question.

No evidence can be found of any reference having been made prior to 1951, of Tommy stealing and spending six months in Durham Jail. It is hard to believe that from the time of the supposed event in 1882, no one would mention it for sixty nine years until WHA first made the allegation in 1951. Tommy, being such a well known character could not have avoided publicity of such an event in the local newspapers. Editors knew Tommy well and were repeatedly publishing 'snippets' about him so would not have missed out on such a golden opportunity to highlight his misfortune.

Anne Armstrong, whose grandfather John Willie Armstrong knew Tommy well, has already been referred to in Chapter 6. John Willie related the following to Anne: Tommy was an honest man who was loved by everyone and his relatives were pleased to help him in his latter years. Honesty was valued in that society so had Tommy stolen from the West Stanley Co-operative Store and been in Durham Jail for six months, his reputation would have been ruined and relatives would not have allowed him to live with them. Following his death, Tommy continued to be held in high regard which would not have been the case if he had been a thief and spent time in prison.

From all available evidence, it would appear that Tommy did not commit theft and did not spend six months in Durham Jail. For reasons best known to himself, WHA chose to make these allegations 31 years after the death of his father.

Chapter 8
REMEMBERING TOMMY

'TOMMY ARMSTRONG MEMORIAL TRUST'
'TOMMY ARMSTRONG SOCIETY'
'OLD MINER TOMMY BEER'

'The Tommy Armstrong Memorial Trust' was founded in March 1986 with the aim of restoring the Tanfield Pitman Poet to his rightful place in the history and culture of the North East.

One of the early tasks undertaken by the Trust was to acquire funding for a replacement memorial gravestone at Tommy's grave in Tanfield Churchyard. On the morning of Saturday the 9th August 1986, the new headstone was unveiled by Arthur Scargill who was then President of the National Union of Mineworkers[1]. The headstone contains the words of the last verse of Tommy's poem 'Durham Strike' which reads:

> The miners of Northumberland we shall ever praise,
> For being so kind in helping us those tyrannising days;
> We thank the other counties too, that have been doing the same,
> For every man who reads will know that we are not to blame.

The Memorial Trust was set up principally to get a book published which allowed the collection of Tommy's works to be brought together. Hence, in 1987, *Polisses and Candymen, The Complete Works of Tommy Armstrong, The Pitman Poet*, edited by Ross Forbes was published by the Trust. At the same time, a cassette tape entitled *Polisses and Candymen* was recorded by a folk group trio – Benny Graham, Bob Fox and Chuck Fleming. The book contained twenty nine of Tommy's works and the cassette tape contained twelve of his songs.

Replacement Headstone erected at Tommy's grave in 1986.

In the words of Ross Forbes, "To be honest, the people behind the Trust weren't great businessmen. The Tommy Armstrong Trust was really just a bunch of us who believed that it was worthwhile to get the book published. The 'business' was run from the Northern Recording Project which was set up during the Miners' Strike. As it transpired, we weren't very good at selling the book or the tape and gave most of them away to people who cared. The Trust was disbanded and we didn't meet many of our aspirations but I had the privilege of working with some great people who all intended to do the right thing. It is a shame to say that some of the moving lights of the Trust are dead now and I must say I miss their cheek and good humour – Derek Little from Stanley and John Kearney from Blackhill in particular. Both were very funny and interesting men."

Over sixty years after the death of Tommy, the formation of this Trust did much to restore his memory and remind people of his importance in the Tanfield Lea area.

'The Tommy Armstrong Society' was formed in 2006 by Gerald Ash (Chairman) and Joe Wilson (Secretary). Gerald, now living at East Boldon, was raised in Tanfield Lea and Joe who lives in the village is a local Councillor. They are both involved in village activities and are keen to perpetuate the memory of Tommy Armstrong, hence the formation of the Society.

Concerts featuring Tommy's songs have been held in St Margaret's Church and the Peacock Public House, both in Tanfield and it is intended that similar events will be arranged. Dr Judith Murphy, a Research Associate at the Northumbria University is an excellent musician and folk singer. She is now the mainstay behind the Concerts and arranges for other artistes to perform with her, all of whom produce a very professional and entertaining evening. At the Peacock public house in 2008, Judith obtained the services of the internationally known folk singer, Jez Lowe and an enjoyable evening was had by all. Two of the performers at each of the Concerts have been the descendants of Tommy's brothers – Elizabeth Armstrong Marshall, descended from Henry Armstrong and Diane Ward, descended from William Wilson Armstrong. To hear their performance of 'Th'Ghost Thit 'Anted Bunty' is a treat to experience.

As explained above, a new headstone was erected at Tommy's grave in 1986 and the

July 2008 – Concert at the Peacock Public House, Tanfield. L to R: Sam Sample (Artiste), Dave Weisser on the PA System, Joe Wilson (Society Secretary) and Judith Murphy (Artiste and Concert Organiser).

original headstone now stands in the churchyard of St Mary Magdalene Church, Trimdon. In view of the history behind the original headstone and how it was funded, arrangements are in hand to have it returned to Tanfield and displayed inside the Parish Church.

In the year 2009, the old stables of Beamish Hall Country House Hotel at Beamish were converted into a public house with restaurant and micro brewery and named 'The Stables'. 'The Tommy Armstrong Society' liaised with Management of the Hotel who agreed to name one of their brewed beers in recognition of the importance of Tommy to the local area. As a result, a photograph of Tommy features on one of the beer pumps at the bar and the beer is named 'Old Miner Tommy'. Patrons at 'The Stables' are therefore drinking to the memory of Tommy. Some will have knowledge of him and others may be interested in finding out about 'Old Miner Tommy'.

The Society has its own Internet Website at:

www.pitmanpoet.derwentside.org.uk

where news of events and other matters affecting the Society can be seen. Tommy would have been amazed at the modern technology and proud to know that, ninety years after his death, his memory lives on through his many compositions.

The members of the Society are doing an excellent job in perpetuating the name of such a notable and wonderful character as Tommy Armstrong and it is hoped that future members of the Society will continue this worthwhile cause.

September 2007 – Concert at St Margaret's Church, Tanfield. Ray Tilly (2nd left) with the three artistes who performed at the concert: L to R: Johnny Handle, Tom Gilfellon and Benny Graham.

The Stables Restaurant at the rear of the Beamish Hall Hotel. Also here is a micro brewery – home of 'Old Miner Tommy'. The Stables opened in May 2009 and, after a lot of suggestions were put forward decided to name one of their beers 'Old Miner Tommy' and approximately 1,000 pints per week are brewed. John Taylor, manager of The Stables Brewery, is also the licensee of the Sun Inn in the 1913 town at Beamish Museum. John's wife, Joanne, can be seen pulling pints by the thousand for the tourists who call into the Sun Inn. A new stronger Pale Ale was introduced in 2010 called 'Tommy's Canny Kyebil'.

The micro brewery at
The Stables Restaurant.

Kamila Ross pulls a pint of 'Old Miner Tommy' at The Stables bar.

PART TWO

WILLIAM HUNTER ARMSTRONG
(1874 – 1953)

William Hunter Armstrong in 1942.

Chapter 9
BIRTH, EDUCATION, THREE MARRIAGES AND ONE DIVORCE

WHA was the third child but the first son of Tommy and his wife Mary Ann (nee Hunter). He was born at Tanfield in 1874 during the reign of Queen Victoria and when he died in 1953, it was just before the Coronation of Queen Elizabeth II. The position of Prime Minister was held by Benjamin Disraeli (Conservative) when WHA was born and Winston Churchill (Conservative) when he died.

The Elementary Education Act 1880, made education compulsory from the ages of five to ten so WHA would have attended school for at least that period of time – circa 1880 to 1885. There was no school in Tanfield Lea until 1890, so he would have walked a mile there and back each day to Tanfield Infant and Church Schools in that adjoining village. The positions he held in later life are a clear indication that he took advantage of and benefitted from the education that was available to him.

Tanfield where WHA attended school.

On the 14th March 1896, WHA married Elizabeth Robson at Stanley Primitive Methodist Chapel and they had two children, Nora Hunter Armstrong and James Armstrong. (See Page 179 for the Family Tree) Descendants of Nora are living in the Scarborough area and those of James are living in the Jarrow/Boldon Colliery area of Tyne & Wear (2010).

Stanley Methodist Church where WHA married Elizabeth Robson.

The marriage to Elizabeth did not last. She started to drink, stay out late at night and get into debt so WHA placed a 'Public Announcement' in the local newspaper in 1905, that he would not be responsible for any debts contracted by her[1]. WHA's wife had a sister who acted as housekeeper for a George McKie in Tantobie and WHA had heard rumours of his wife's relations with McKie. On returning home unexpectedly one day, WHA found McKie in his house and when he remonstrated with his wife, she retorted that she could have a home in McKie's house whenever she liked. A few days later, she left WHA and went to live with McKie at Tantobie where it was said that she and her sister were living with McKie as though he had two wives. In 1909 at the Royal Courts of Justice in London, WHA was granted a divorce on the grounds that his wife had habitually committed adultery with George McKie. WHA was granted custody of the two children Nora and James[2].

After his divorce from his first wife, WHA married Annie Lightfoot at the Primitive Methodist Church at Gateshead on the 9th March 1910. Annie was a widow with a daughter Mary Ann P. Lightfoot who later married Ralph Waggitt and they continued to live in the village of Tanfield Lea. In later years, Annie who was nine years older than WHA, became an invalid and was wheelchair bound. About 1940, Agnes Moir who was a widow with a son William Alexander Moir (Alex), moved into WHA's home as a housekeeper and carer for his invalid wife. His wife died in June 1941 but Agnes and Alex Moir remained in the home of WHA.

*Part of West Street, Tanfield Lea where WHA lived at Number One –
being demolished in the mid 1960s.*

In May 1942, by which time he was aged sixty seven and she was six
months pregnant by him, WHA married Agnes Moir at Stanley
Methodist Church. In August 1942, Agnes gave birth to a boy, Norman
Armstrong, but sadly the poor little thing died six days later in the
Maternity Hospital. After the death of WHA in 1953, his widow Agnes
continued to live in the village of Tanfield Lea until her death in 1988.

*6 Memorial Homes, Tanfield Lea where WHA lived at the time of his
death in 1953.*

Chapter 10
ANECDOTES

Katherine Beaumont is the widow of Alex Moir (1932-2005) who was the stepson of WHA. Whilst Katherine never met WHA, Alex told her various anecdotes about WHA, the following of which are examples:

WHA always referred to Alex as 'the boy' and Alex had to call him Mr Armstrong.

WHA was deeply involved with the Primitive Methodist Church and the Minister used to call at their home from time to time. On one such occasion, they were about to have lunch and invited the Minister to join them. Alex noticed some maggots on the meat and whispered this fact to his mother Agnes. She told him to keep quiet about it and the meal went off without the Minister or WHA apparently noticing the maggots.

Money was short so Alex's mother Agnes had to ensure that WHA had the main share of the meat at mealtimes whilst she and Alex had what was left.

In his later years, WHA was quite deaf, had little conversation and rarely spoke to Alex directly; it was invariably through his mother. An example was at the meal table when WHA would say to Agnes, "Ask the boy if he wants a slice of bread." Agnes would then ask the question of Alex and relay the answer to WHA.

Alex spent three years in the Royal Air Force. In 1963, he moved to London where he was involved in theatre management and acting. He had small parts in films including *Camp on Blood Island* and *The Day The Earth Caught Fire*. He also had parts in the television series, *Z Cars* and *Emergency Ward Ten*.

Ivan Garnham, now living in Stanley, is a retired Headmaster of Tanfield Lea Junior School. Ivan remembers WHA

Alex Moir.

very well and was also able to relate some anecdotes about WHA.

Ivan as a Cadet in the Order of the Sons of Temperance Society became a 'Worthy Archon' and in 1939 was presented with a Certificate by WHA who was Patron of the Society.

WHA was a keen bowls player and used to play in Tanfield Lea Welfare Park.

Ivan recalled that WHA was knocked down by a motor car. A local newspaper which reported that event[1] in 1939, explained that WHA had just left Woodside Methodist Church when he was knocked down and taken to his home. The Doctor was summoned and found WHA to be suffering from fractured ribs and general shock.

When Ivan was a youngster in the village of Tanfield Lea, he and everyone else always looked up to WHA who was a 'pillar of society'.

The 'Cadets of Temperance' certificate presented to Ivan Garnham by WHA in 1939.

Gerald Ash was raised in Tanfield Lea and lived in Sydney Terrace. Gerald recalls that WHA was an enthusiastic gardener with an allotment at the end of Sydney Terrace. He maintained that enthusiasm up to his latter days and when WHA became old and frail, Gerald used to see him being pushed along in a wheelbarrow to his allotment by his wife Agnes. She used to push him along the avenue between Sydney Terrace and Jutland Terrace.

Chapter 11
WORK, UNION AND WELFARE ACTIVITIES

When aged eleven, WHA started work at Tanfield Lea Colliery, known as Margaret Colliery. Based on his obituary, when he retired at the age of sixty five, he had given fifty four years service to the coal mining industry, all underground and all at Tanfield Lea Colliery[1]. Many of those years were as a hewer, which at that time involved hacking away at the coal face with a hand held pick.

Tanfield Lea Colliery.

He had a long involvement with Tanfield Lea Miners' Lodge of the Durham Miners' Association and filled numerous official positions including many years as Secretary. In the 'Award & Agreements' records for Tanfield Lea Colliery, WHA features on many occasions as representing the 'Workmen' in negotiations with the 'Owners' from 1920 to 1937[2]. Two examples of his negotiations on behalf of the workmen were: i) "Agreeing alterations in the hewing prices in various parts of the Colliery in 1920", and ii) "Owners of the Colliery wanting prices and conditions fixed for Hand Putting and Pony Putting with steel tubs in 1937."

In November 1938, along with many others, he was presented with a Diploma for fifty years loyalty to the Trade Union which means he had been a member since at least the age of thirteen. The presentation was made by Will Lawther, Vice President of the Mineworkers' Federation of Great Britain[3].

Colliery Offices, Tanfield Lea. 3887

Tanfield Lea Colliery Offices.

In 1929, the Tanfield Lea Colliery Welfare Committee was formed and WHA was appointed Vice Chairman[4]. At the annual meeting on the 24th January 1931, he was elected as Chairman[5]. He was also Chairman of the Welfare Bowls Club and unfortunately in that capacity, made a slip up with a letter to the local newspaper in 1946[6]. The Club had won the Mid-Week Section Cup of the North-West Durham Bowling League but the Cup was not there to be presented, nor was there any official present. In his letter to the newspaper, WHA raised query about this fact which prompted a curt reply from the Chairman and the Secretary of the Bowling League in the following week's newspaper[7]. They pointed out that if Tanfield Lea had been represented at the last meeting of the League Committee to which they were invited, they would have known of the unanimous decision to present the Cup to the winners at the forthcoming Annual General Meeting. Sensibly, WHA did not pursue the matter in subsequent newspapers and presumably they were presented with the Cup at the Annual General Meeting.

As well as spending all his working life in the coal mine, WHA gave an enormous amount of time in representing and pursuing the well being of his fellow workmen. Even after he retired, he was quick to speak up in support of the workers as he did in the following letter published in the local newspaper in 1948[8]:

NATIONAL INSURANCE ACT

Sir, – May I say a word or two on the above Act. While the Act will be welcomed by working people, the administration of this scheme (especially in our area, Stanley and District, whose Headquarters are at Gateshead) is shocking.

I will quote one instance out of the many in Tanfield Lea area. A young man was off work sick two weeks; he has been working six weeks and had not received his money on Friday last, even after his mother wrote to Gateshead. Doctor's Certificates were sent in. Why should any mother or wife have to write for the money that is due? In Northumberland, I suppose every penny due is paid at the proper time. It makes us wonder if they are all indifferent at the head office, Gateshead. In any case, management like this neither helps the Labour Party; and certainly not those who are unfortunate to be off sick.

I trust something will be done to impose matters in this area or otherwise the Minister of Insurance must be asked to deal with the question.

W.H. ARMSTRONG
Tanfield Lea

WHA was also keen to express appreciation as shown in the following letter published in the local newspaper in 1946[9]:

TANFIELD LEA COLLIERY COMFORTS

Sir, – On behalf of the 108 men from the above colliery who went into the Forces, I have to thank all the workmen and officials for their splendid gifts during the war and since. The letters from all of them have been inspiring, in fact, words couldn't express their appreciation. Eleven of them made the supreme sacrifice. It's marvellous what one penny per week kept off at the colliery office has meant. The sum raised was £781 5s 3d and sums have been sent periodically to the lads. Some got over £7 and others less; this was determined by when they joined up. It's a truism "That many can help one, whereas one may not help many." May I express the thanks of both those who contributed one penny per week, and those who received the benefits; and to the bill clerks for keeping this large sum off the pay notes without commission. This was done from 2nd February 1940 to 9th November 1945. There's nothing cheaper than appreciation and yet there's nothing appreciated more.

Wm. H. ARMSTRONG
(Fin. Sec. and Treas.)

There is no doubt that WHA did much to help others and was enthusiastically involved with activities to benefit the village of Tanfield Lea.

Chapter 12
THE CHURCH AND OTHER ACTIVITIES

An Obituary in the local newspaper in 1953 includes the following summary of WHA's association with Woodside Primitive Methodist Church[1]:

"Mr Armstrong was a prominent figure in local Methodist circles and he was usually referred to as the 'Father' of the Woodside Methodist Church, with which he had been associated for 59 years. Interested in the work of all departments of the church, he was a trustee and for a number of years filled the position of Superintendent of the Sunday School."

At the annual festival of the church during the August Bank Holiday in 1913, Maypole performances were provided by the children. The performances reflected much credit on the trainers, one of whom was WHA[2].

Maypole Performance Group with WHA standing in the centre at the back.

Tanfield Lea Woodside Methodist Church Sunday School Anniversary in 1949. Front Row left to right: Billy Buglass, Gerald Ash, Alex Moir and Billy Oglenby. All the adults standing behind the boys were Sunday School Teachers.

As one of the Leaders of the church, he often featured in the Minutes of the Leaders Meetings and stood in as Chairman when the Reverend G.H. Parbrook was absent. At the meeting on the 21st May 1942, his letter of resignation was 'accepted with regret'[3]. It may be that his resignation had something to do with his marriage to Agnes Moir on the 9th May that year and who was already six months pregnant by WHA.

As well as his long association with the church, WHA was involved with other activities in and around the village of Tanfield Lea as follows:

i) A Committee Member of West Stanley Co-operative Society from May 1915 to August 1919[4].

ii) President of the South Ward of the Tanfield Urban Area Nursing Association when it was granted affiliation to the Durham County Nursing Association in 1920[5].

iii) He was an enthusiastic gardener and was an Official with Tanfield Lea Gardening Association[1].

iv) In 1949, the Tanfield Lea Branch of the Old Aged Pensioners Association was formed by WHA, his wife Agnes and four other couples with WHA as Secretary. After the inaugural meeting, there were musical items including Tommy's song 'Th' Borth e' th' Lad' sung by WHA[6].

v) He also wrote some poems and details of this activity are shown later in Part Six.

Opening of Tanfield Lea Memorial Institute in 1925. The man in the front row, third from the left with his hand slotted inside his overcoat is Timothy Armstrong, a nephew of Tommy — son of Tommy's older brother William Wilson Armstrong. Timothy was Mayor of Gateshead for the two successive years of 1933 and 1934.

THE ORDER OF THE SONS OF TEMPERANCE SOCIETY (SOT)

In September 1842, The Order of the Sons of Temperance Society was founded in New York and in November 1849, the first Division in England was formed in Liverpool and named 'Queens No. 1 Division'. The aims of the Society were twofold; first to promote total abstinence from alcohol and second to provide insurance benefits for persons who abstained. Fortnightly contributions were made for benefits in the event of sickness through accident or in the event of death[7]. In the years that followed, Divisions of the SOT were formed throughout Great Britain and Ireland.

On the 7th October 1904 at the age of twenty nine, WHA joined the 'Hope of White-le-Head Sub-Division'. Being a strong advocate of temperance and having an avid desire for the advancement of SOT, he was elected as Patron the following year[8]. As a result of his efforts and determination, Tanfield Lea acquired its own Sub-Divisional status in May 1908, became known as 'The Hope of Tanfield Lea' and WHA was appointed Worthy Patron[9].

Due to his keen and ardent interest in the 'Grand Division of Newcastle upon Tyne', he was rewarded for his services by being elected to the Management Committee in 1912. WHA moved further up in office until February 1923 when he was bestowed with the highest position of honour in the Grand Division, that of Grand Worthy Patriarch, a position which was held for one year only[8]. In honour of this appointment, the 'Hope of Tanfield Lea Division' presented him with a writing desk at their meeting in March 1923[10].

He also worked hard to encourage youngsters to join the Cadet Section of SOT at Tanfield Lea. Some who were members, still live in and around the village and can relate anecdotes about WHA's almost fanaticism against alcohol, such as "It's not the last glass of whisky that kills you, it's the first glass." At a concert in the village in March 1921, three of the Cadets performed a sketch called 'The Value of Section Work' which had been composed by WHA and was printed in the March 1921 issue of the magazine 'Cadet of Temperance'[11]. Unfortunately, the magazine has not survived.

It is apparent from the Minutes of the Management Committee of Newcastle Grand Division, that WHA was deeply involved with and held in high regard by that office. As a Committee Member, on behalf of the Grand Division he used to visit Divisions which were experiencing difficulties to encourage them in their endeavours. On occasions, instead of having its Quarterly Meeting in Newcastle, the Grand Division would hold the meeting at one of the Divisions. When this occurred, a number of the Committee Members, accompanied by the local Salvation Army Band, used to parade through the streets. They would stop at various points where WHA would deliver a short address about the evils of alcohol. Some of the places where they paraded were Lemington, Ashington and Grange Villa[12].

After a long and distinguished association with the Newcastle upon Tyne Grand Division of the SOT, WHA resigned in February 1945. However, he continued as Patron of the 'Hope of Tanfield Lea Division' until his death in 1953[12].

Woodside Primitive Methodist Church and Church Hall, Tanfield Lea where the Sons of Temperance held meetings.

Chapter 13
RELATIONSHIP AND ILLEGITIMATE SON

WHA's involvement with the Order of the Sons of Temperance Society (SOT) has been explained in an earlier chapter. Another Division of the SOT was the Progressive Division which held its meetings in the Primitive Methodist Church in Jubilee Avenue, Eighton Banks. Margaret Annie Eliza Tilly (Maggie), was the Organist and on various Committees at the Church[1]. She was also a representative of the Progressive Division of SOT and attended meetings of the SOT Grand Division in Newcastle upon Tyne[2].

Whilst WHA and Maggie were at the Newcastle meetings, their friendship developed resulting in Maggie visiting Tanfield Lea to help care for WHA's second wife Annie who was an invalid and confined to a wheelchair. It was during these visits that the friendship of WHA and Maggie developed into a relationship, as a result of which Maggie became pregnant[3]. At this time WHA was fifty nine and Maggie was thirty two, having been born in 1901 which was the same year in

Margaret A.E. Tilly as a young girl with her parents and three brothers in 1906.

which WHA's son James was born. On the 26th August 1934, Maggie gave birth to her illegitimate son by WHA. The registration of the boy's birth and his baptism were both in the name Raymond Wilfred Tilly (Ray). Neither the birth nor the baptism certificates contained the name of his father.

As Maggie then had to look after her baby, she could no longer help care for WHA's invalid wife. The Electoral Registers suggest that WHA had 'live in carers' to help with his wife – Susan M. Sanders in 1936 and Sarah J. Stewart in 1939. In 1940, Agnes Moir moved in with her son Alex.

Until he was about six, Ray remembers his mother Maggie taking him to Tanfield Lea on a few occasions but cannot remember who they visited. Whether Maggie was taking Ray to see WHA or anyone else at Tanfield Lea is not known but these visits stopped about the time when WHA's invalid wife died and Agnes Moir was living at his home.

It could not have been easy for Maggie to cope with what was in those days, the stigma of having an illegitimate son and the financial hardships that followed. Ray had a very happy and caring upbringing by his mother Maggie and her parents at Eighton Banks. He never knowingly met WHA and WHA never contributed either financially or in any other way towards his illegitimate son.

Margaret A.E. Tilly with her brother Wilfred outside Buckingham Palace in September 1941 when he was presented with the British Empire Medal for gallantry.

CONCLUSION

When I discovered the identity of my father, WHA and grandfather, Tommy, I launched into my research with great enthusiasm. As a general rule, family historians are pleased to discover there are 'skeletons in the cupboard' about their ancestors, so when I learnt that in Tommy, I supposedly had an ancestral felon and drunkard, I wanted to find out everything about the circumstances of these events. I knew that in particular, local newspaper reports would be most helpful in that respect.

However, the more I delved into Tommy, the more I began to doubt the truthfulness of the stories. Now, based on all I have learnt during my research, I am convinced that Tommy did not steal pit stockings from the Co-operative Store at West Stanley, nor did he spend six months in Durham Jail. Similarly, I am convinced that Tommy's drinking habits have been grossly exaggerated to suggest that he was a drunkard.

The initial suggestions that Tommy was either a thief or a drunkard emanate from his son WHA. Being a staunch teetotaller and with the experience of his first wife who took to drink, it is perhaps not surprising that WHA was against alcohol. However, he became intolerant towards anyone who drank any alcohol at all, including his father and he also influenced the views of others about Tommy.

As for why WHA would allege, wrongly, that his father Tommy had committed theft and spent six months in Durham Jail, I have no idea. What I do know of course is that WHA had a 'skeleton in his cupboard', which was me. I wonder if anyone else is still alive who remembers my being the result of a relationship between WHA and my mother Margaret A.E. Tilly.

Readers of this book must form their own conclusions about the answers to the two questions I raised in my Introduction. Was my grandfather, Thomas Armstrong, the drunkard and criminal he is alleged to have been? And, was my father, William Hunter Armstrong, the completely moral upstanding figure in his community that we understand from contemporary reports of the time?

PART THREE

Thirty Previously Published Works of Thomas Armstrong

Twenty five of these were published by his son WHA in 1909, in the first edition of the 'Song Book' of Tommy's works and repeated in the next two editions. Those and another five of his works have since appeared in a number of publications.

An 'Introduction' at the beginning of each poem gives any known details relevant to the work.

THE BLANCHLAND MURDER

Robert Snowball lived with his father and a housekeeper, Jane Baron, at Belmont Farm near Blanchland. Robert had a room above the byre which he used as a carpenter's shop. He went out on New Years Day – 1st January 1880 but did not return that night. Next day, he was found dead in his carpenter's shop having been struck on the back of his head with a large hammer[1].

Armstrong wrote this poem, presumably within a few days of the death because on the 27th January 1880, the housekeeper was charged with the murder. However, when she appeared at Durham Assizes on the 17th April 1880, she was acquitted.

WHILE looking thro' the papers at my home the other day,
I saw there'd been a murder in a cruel and barb'rous way.
About two miles from Blanchland, old Snowball and his son
Did occupy the Belmont Farm, where the murder has been done.
This young man, Robert Snowball, from his home did go away,
And join'd some friends at Blanchland to spend the New Year's Day;
He came home in the afternoon, but did not long remain;
Some neighbours still he wished to see, so he went out again.

Chorus:
Young and old take my advice, and keep from doing harm;
Just think of the cruel murder that's been done at Belmont Farm.

At twelve o'clock he had not come, so then the father said
Unto Jane Baron, the housekeeper, "I think I'll go to bed;
Perhaps he has joined with some friends, and may be out till late."
"Yes, you can go to bed," said she, "and I will of him wait."
Next morning when the father rose he began to sigh and fret,
When she told him that his dear son had not returned home yet:
"I waited lonely by myself till three o'clock this morn,
I thought I need no longer wait, as he did not return."

Chorus

A quantity of blood was found while looking in the byre,
Where it came from the old man then began to enquire;
Ascending to the room above, o'er him there came a dread
The first thing that his eyes fell on was his son Robert – dead.
The tears came trickling down his cheeks, as near his son he stood.
A hammer also stood close by, bespattered o'er with blood.
We hope that God in heaven will not let the murderer rest;
We trust that Robert Snowball's soul is mingled with the blest.

Chorus

BOBBY AND BET

Tommy Armstrong wrote this poem and as he used to write about people living in Tanfield Lea and the surrounding area, it is possible that Bob & Betty Nicholson were local residents.

BOB NICHOLSON alwis like't his beer, their Betty wis fond iv hor gin;
They had ne bairns te bother thor lives, an' nebody used to gan in.
Bob wis a regular quiet man, their Betty wis quite the revarse;
Aw've heerd folks say the Devil wis bad, but Bob swore Betty wis warse.

Chorus:
So Bobby an' Bet wis exactly met, to pairt them it wad be a shem;
For if Bob gets drunk it th' public hoose, their Betty gets drunk it yem.

Bob went one neet an' gat mortil drunk their Betty cried oot for shem;
He wis lying drunk ipon the road, an' she wis drunk it yem.
She jump't off hor seat en on tive hor feet, wi' the candil an' knife iv
  hor hands,
For te cut a bit meat for Bobby te eat, but sh' didn't knaw wen he wid
  land.

Chorus

She cut the meat an' fetch't the plate, an' started te scrum the pan oot;
She torn'd that duzzie, she fell back ower, sh' had te leeve go iv the cloot.
"Aw's clivvor," sh' sais, so she put off hor clais she showt thit she'd
  finished hor job –
Thor wis nowt but the dish cloot left i' the pan, an' a forst-rate supper
  for Bob.

Chorus

Wen Bob com yem he teuk off his claes, he thowt she'd fried him sum
  pork;
So he clapt the dish-cloot on te the plate, an' luck'd for his knife an' fork.
He started te eat his little bit meat, "My word, but," he sais, "it's teuf,
The butchor's either muaid a mistake, or else it isn't eneuf."

Chorus

Bob jumpt on the flor an' cursed an' swor, thit his supper wid cawse
  his deeth;
There wis lumps ev cloot the size o' me airm stickin between his teeth.
He nearly went mad wi' the suppor he'd had, he wisht awl the
  butchors wis deed;
He teuk up the scissors an' went te their Bet an' cut awl the hair off
  hor heed.

Spoken: Betty's joined the Blue Ribbon Army an drinks nowt but bittor beer; she sais gin used te muaik hor drunk.

TH' BORTH E TH' LAD

This was probably the first poem written by Tommy Armstrong – in
1864 when he was aged fifteen or sixteen². Even at that early age,
Tommy's creativity comes to the fore as he describes his own birth. It is
still popular as a song amongst folk singers today.

Aw'll de me best to please ye, en th' best cin de ne mair,
Aw's gan te sing eboot mesel-wen aw wis born, en wair;
Aw wis born at Shotley, aw've ard me muther sae,
Twis in th' munth iv August, en on th' fifteenth dae.

Spoken: Aw cin mind that mornen aw wis born is if it wis th' neet. Th'
pits wis aul idle th' next dae – because it wis Sunda'; but ye wadn't
thout it wis Sunda' it wor hoose. Thor wis that much tee en gingor beer
drunken aw wis forst te stop th' tap. Dolly Potts got tite en flung a
saucer it Betty Green, but it mist hor en catcht me between th' ies en
mooth, en aw've ad a greet lump thare ivor since. But we seun muaid
hor en ootside passengor, en we ingoid worselves we singen -

Chorus: *He is the best iv ony,*
                     For his fuaice it is se bonny,
                     We'll caul 'im Tommy,
                     Hees th' pictor iv hees dad;
                     So th' popt on th' kettil,
                     Is seun is things wis settled,
                     En th' tee wis fettild,
                     Ower th' borth e th' lad.

Aw mind it was warm wethor wen thae receev'd this lad,
Me fethor danc'd ipon th' flor te show thit he wis glad;
Me muthor she lae smilen, en cauld me be me nuaim,
She sais, "God bless thee little heart, aw's plees'd thoo's landed yem."

Spoken: Ye naw thae expected me three munth before that (aw's e
twelve munth bairn – but ye can see that be me size). That wis th' forst
time aw seed Betty Lee, th' mid-wife. She tuek me up en lade me ecross
hor nee, en said te me muthor, "Aw think aw'll wesh im." Aw thowt
she sade, "Aw think aw'll thresh im" – aw teuk hor up rang. If she'd
lade e finger on me aw wid guain strite back te wair aw cam freh. Aw
gat e gud wesh en e nue sute on, en we started te sing.

Chorus

Th' neibors com te brickfast, this nue-born bairn te see,
Mistres Wite gat mortal drunk we drinken Stewart's tee;
Miss Watson wis religyis, en so wis Mistris Kae,
En is seun is deun we brickfast, th' buaith nelt doon te prae.

Spoken: Th' brickfast wis 'ardly ower te thae doon on te thor nees en began te prae it th' top e thor voise. Is suen is thae startid to prae, aw started te sing "Johnny cums marchin' hoam." It wis a great favourite e mine at that time. Nan Watson shooted tiv aud Betty Lee, th' mid-wife, "Stop that child from crien, or I must cease praying"; and Betty shoots, "Get ewae wi thou; th' bairn's not cryen – hee's singen; th' bairn naws is weel is me thoo's prayen e cheet, so thoo'd better get on te thee feet en sing, esteed e prayen."

Chorus

"My word," said Mistris Robson, is she lade me on hor airm.
"Iv aul me time aw nivor met we such t witey bairn."
Th' doctor just had landed, so aw sees'd 'im be th' cote,
But littil wair thae thinking thit th' bairn wis e pote.

Spoken: Is seun is ivor th' doctor com within th' dor, aw grab'd 'im be th' neck, en aw didint forget to shaik 'im; but ye naw aw wis e vary big lad wen aw wis littil. Aw axt 'im hoo he wid like to stop in prison three munth eftor hees time wis up but we seun gat aul reet – en me fethor wissil'd; Betty en th' doctor danc'd to cloasen time. Aw wis sair we laffin, so we finished we singen –

Chorus

A young lad ready for bathtime.

THE CAT PIE

This poem was written by Tommy sometime after 1888 when Jack Coxon became Landlord of the Stanley Inn, Brewery Square, Stanley. Jack's wife Bessie was annoyed about her home made pies being constantly taken from her pantry and was determined to put a stop to it. She got Jack and his friend Bob Charlton to shoot a cat which she made into a pie. The three culprits fell for the bait and devoured the pie. When the news got out, they were forever greeted with mews and cat calls[3].

THORE'S been a grand dinnor not far frae Sheel Raw,
At a place th' call Stanley, for testen th' jaw;
Tiv a hoose ivory Sunda' sum cheps used to gan,
An' eat all th' meat thit wis boil l' th' pan.

> *Chorus:*
> *Fal th' dal laddie*
> *Sing fal the dal day*
> *Fal the dal laddie*
> *Sing fal the dal day*

These chaps used to gan an' sit doon on a seat,
Thae knew thit Jack alwis had plenty i' meat;
But Coxon an' Charlton went oot for te try
Te catch an awd cat for te muaik them a pie.

> *Chorus*

Th' cat thit thae gat wis elivon eer awd,
Thae knew w' th' pie thit these cheps wad be glad;
So thae kill'd it, an' clean'd it, an' teuk off each lim.
When th' pie wis awl riddy thae shoved pussy in.

> *Chorus*

Th' cat being se awd, thae thowt 'twad be dry,
So thae put potted heed in te gravy th' pie,
Then into th' yuven th' pie wis then put,
Th' yuven wis het an' th' door wis kept shut.

> *Chorus*

Wen th' pie wis awl riddy an' nicely keukt,
Into th' pantry Bob Charlton then teukt;
Th' crust he broke into se cunnen an' sly,
Te muaik them believe they'd been eaten' th' pie.

> *Chorus*

So in cums Joe Peel, Joe Witfield, an' Bob,
Like other times, thae wor ment for th' gob;
Bob Charlton then whispered te Witfield se slee :
"If thoo lucks i' th' pantry a pie thoo can see."

Chorus

Thae thowt 'twis a rabbit, an hoo te muaik thares,
Charlton gat Coxon te gan up th' stairs;
Bob Witfield then thowt a grand trick he wad try
So he into th' pantry an' off wi' th' pie.

Chorus

He off alang th' Raw an' doon intiv a field,
He thowt he'd deun clivor th' pie for te steal;
Him an' Joe Peel se contentedly sat,
Enjoyen thorsels wi' th' lims iv a cat.

Chorus

Charlton an' Coxon buaith laft fit to bust;
Te see them on chewen th' cat an' th' crust;
Joe Peel gat a leg thit he thowt wis eneuf,
He sais, "Bob, it's nice, but it's terable teuf."

Chorus

Thae eat sum iv pussy, an' drove a bit crack,
Until thae agreed for te tuaik th' pie back;
Wen thae gat to th' hoose, thae went at it aguain,
Till in th' pie dish thor wis ardly a buain.

Chorus

Ye wad a laft if ye'd only been in,
Wen Bob Charlton held up befor them th' skin;
As seun is th' skin e th' pussy thae saw,
Thae ran te th' dor an' thae started to thraw.

Chorus

Th' cat wis awl eaten, but just th' cat skin,
But it wad been eaten had thae puten't in;
Poor pussy it's guain, but thor's men iv its place,
Th' mice dorsent luck these young cheps in e th' face.

CONSETT CHOIR CALAMITY

On the afternoon of Saturday the 26th August 1911, a char-a-banc was carrying 33 members of the Consett Co-operative Choir to Prudhoe to take part in an annual choral competition. On descending a steep twisting hill known as Long Close Bank near Medomsley, the brake failed and in spite of every effort by the driver, the vehicle crashed into a tree on a sharp bend whilst travelling at about sixty miles per hour. Ten of the passengers were killed in the accident and twenty others were injured[4]. Tommy Armstrong wrote this poem to commemorate the tragic accident.

The char-a-banc on an occasion prior to being used to transport the choir.

Scripture tells us very plain to "Think not of to-morrow,"
Because our happiness and joys may quickly turn to sorrow.
How many cases have we known up to the present time
Where Death has called away young men and women in their prime.
Some we knew that suffered long in bed, both night and day,
And others, in the best of health, were suddenly called away.
When the appointed time has come, to Death we cannot say;
I'm not prepared to go just yet, call back some future day.

Death will take no bribery, or one thing would be sure,
The Rich would live, and Death would only call upon the poor.
We know there's danger everywhere, no matter where we go,
Look at the sad calamity – going to Prudhoe Show.
A happy band of Vocalists from Consett went away,
To join a Singing Competition which was held that day.
The vehicle which they'd engaged at Consett did arrive,
The weather was both fine and fair, and pleasant for a drive.

The vehicle with its passengers which numbered twenty-eight,
Delayed no time at Consett, lest they should be too late;
A pleasant smile was on each face, all hearty and so gay,
They all joined in with one accord, to sing while on their way;
They sang with voices loud and sweet, in praise of God on high;
But little thought that afternoon that some of them would die.
Death was riding with them, but little did they know,
That not a one amongst the lot would see the Prudhoe Show.

When they arrived at Medomsley, five passengers were there,
Waiting for to join their friends, their pleasures for to share;
The vehicle stopped and took them in, they each one took their seat,
They moved away, but never thought of danger, or the troubles they
    would meet.
All went well until they reached a bank both steep and long,
On going down it could be seen that there was something wrong;
The vehicle ran much faster than what it ought to go;
The danger that their lives were in not one of them did know.

The driver did his very best, the vehicle for to guide,
Thinking of the passengers that he had got inside;
The brake refused to do its work, none of the company knew,
The driver sat and did his best to bring them safely through;
There was no chance of jumping out 'twas useless for to try,
They had no other chance but sit, which made their end so nigh;
And when he had lost all control – exhausted as could be –
The vehicle and its passengers ran smash into a tree.

As soon as the disaster, the news was quickly spread
That twenty-five were injured, and nine were lying dead;
The ambulance and doctors too, were soon upon the ground
With stimulants and bandages to dress up each one's wound.
One young man named Pearson, was injured so that day,
On going to the Infirmary, he died upon the way.
We hope those Ten have landed save into the Home above,
Where all is Happiness, and Peace, and Everlasting love.

The char-a-banc following the crash.

CORRY'S RAT

This poem was written by Tommy Armstrong and has previously been published in various places. Corry's Rat is referred to in the comical letter from Tommy when he was living at Whitley Bay – See Chapter 3.

> IT wis hiteen sivinty, th' twentv-forst e Mae,
> Me en Harry Gibson will not forget th' dae;
> Wen aw wis bissy shiften ewae freh Eden Plaice
> Up te little Tanfield – but ye shill heer me caise.

Spoken: Wen ye heer me sad story, aw wadint be sorprised te see th' teers run doon yor cheeks th' size e cocoanuts; aw cud crie ivory time aw think eboot it; aw wad, tee, but aw's flade onybody sees me, so aw'll just sing ye a ditty.

> *Chorus:*
> *"Stop 'em thare, catch "em," thae awl began te shoot;*
> *Th' driver en hees passingors aul com tumilen oot;*
> *If ivor aw shud shift eguain, aw'll shift them we me hat,*
> *Aw'll nivor more be flade to deed we Mistor Corry's rat.*

Spoken: Aw's e terribil chep for floor shoas, but thae alwis heh thim e th' rang plaice; thae shud heh thim e th' tap room – that wid just suite Tommy Martin en me; but thor's gan te be nowt but pultry it th' next floor show; be shoor en cum, en aw'll sing ye –

> *Chorus*

> We started then e shiften, we shifted fower lode,
> E cumen doon aw saw sum bards sitten on th' rode;
> Thae wor sitten feeden, th' rat thae nivor seed,
> So thae aul floo up tegither on thae flade th' rat te deed.

Spoken: Aw saw e flock e sparrows geten thor brickfist off sum muck thit sum e th' horses left lyen on th' rode. Thae nivor stord te we gat reet te them, en off thae went, en so did sum body else; th' bords floo nee sharper than th' rat went. so aw started te sing –

> *Chorus*

> Th' galewae lade hees lugs back, en cockt hees tail up tee,
> Aw saw be hees ippeerince thit he wis gan te flee;
> Aw was th' forst thit tumild oot – aw fell emang th' weeIs
> Ye wide laft if ye'd been thare, te see me coup me creels.

Spoken: Ye tuak eboot yor mountybanks tornin summorsets en dabing on thor feet! Aw divint naw hoo mony times aw torned ower, but aw wis ganen ower th' sivinth time wen aw lost me senses. Aw mite gan ower mony e time eftor that, but a dabd on me heed en noct aul th' wull off th' top. Wen aw com eroond aw started te sing –

Aw teuk me left leg e me hand, en did me best te wauk.
Wen aw fell in we Harry he ad ardly strength te tauk;
Th' blood wis runnen doon hees fuaice – 'twis pitiful te see –
En wen aw tried te lift 'im up, he sade, "O let me be,"

Spoken: Poor Harry! aw wis sorry for 'im, he wis shoor te be stupified
– we th' sharp ride en th' sudint stop. If th' rat had been runen for th'
Derby; it wid been like King Charles – it wid guain fors past th' post we
nee jock on its back; poor me, th'e jock, was lyen ootside th' ring
singen –

Chorus

Hee's fuaice wis full e scratches; he sais, "Aw've smasht me rist."
Aw told him if we'd buiath been kild we nivor wad been mist.
Then Mistress Watson at th' Farm she cried oot "What's th'
mattor?"
Aw sais, "Plees, ma'am, just be se kind is fetch e drink e wattor."

Spoken: Aw sade wattor, but aw ment whisky; but she browt wattor.
Aw tost it aul ower hees heed en fuaice, en wen aw browt nim eboot
we started te sing –

Chorus

Thanks te Mistor Emory, the mesmorisem man,
For stoppen Corry's galewae he had e clivor plan;
He stopt it in e moment, en th' fokes began to stare.
En thanks te Mistor Corry, but aw'll hev hees rat nee mare.

Spoken: He saw th' rat cumen, en he set hiself e th' middle e th' rode
en shooted, "Fixt – you can't stor." It wis troo; it stud tiv aw teuk im be
th' heed, en aw teukt yem backwards; aw muaid e Hale-e-loo-lye on
im –

Chorus

A speedy rat.

DORHAM JAIL

This poem was written by Tommy Armstrong. A 'myth', initiated by his son William Hunter Armstrong, alleged that it was based on Tommy's actual experience of Durham Gaol where he was sentenced to six months for stealing a pair of pit stockings from the Co-operative Store at West Stanley[5]. As it made a 'good story', it was perpetuated and exaggerated by various writers to include such comments as:- he was drunk at the time; from the way they were displayed, the stockings looked bow-legged; they were the only bow-legged stockings he had seen; as he was small and bow-legged the stockings seemed ideal for him.

As good a story as this might make, it is not true. This work was one of Tommy's fun poems like 'Tommy the Poet Signed On' and others. Tommy was never convicted of stealing and never spent six months in Durham Gaol. See 'Chapter 7: CONTROVERSIES'.

YIL awl hev ard O' Dorham Jail, but it wad ge much sorprise
To see th' prisoners in th' yard, wen thay'r on exorsise,
This yard is bilt eroond we walls, se noabil en see strang,
We ivor gans thae heh te bide thor time, be it short or lang.

> *Chorus:*
> *And thare's nee gud luck in Dorham Jail thare's nee gud luck it awl;*
> *Wat is breed en skilly for but just te muaik ye smaul?*

Wen ye gan to Dorham Jail thae'll find ye wiv emploi,
Thae'll dress ye up se dandy in a suit e cordy-roy;
Thae'll fetch e cap wivout e peek, en nivor axe yor size,
En, like yor suite, its cordy-roy, en cums doon ower yor ies.

> *Chorus*

Th' forst munth is th' warst iv awl your feelens thae will trie;
There's nowt but two greet lumps e wood, on which ye heh to lie.
Then eftor that ye get e bed, but it is ard is stuains;
It neet ye dorsint muaik e torn, for feer ye brick sum buains.

> *Chorus*

Awl kines e wark there's ganen on upon these noable flats,
Teesin oakim, muaiken balls, en weeven coco mats.
Wen ye gan in ye mae be thin, but thae cin muaik ye thinnor;
If your oakim is not teesed, thae'r shoor to stop yor dinnor.

> *Chorus*

Th' shoos ye get is oftin tens, th' smaulist size is nine;
Tho'r big eneugh to muaik a skiff for Boyd ipon th' Tyne.
En if ye shud be caud at neets, just muaik yorsels at yem;
Lap yor clais eroond yor shoos, en get inside e them.

Chorus

Yil get yor meat en clais for nowt, yor hoose en firin' free;
Awl yor meet's browt te th' dor hoo happy ye shud be!
Thor's soap en too'l en wooden speun, en a little bairne's pot;
Thae fetch yor papers ivory week for ye te clean your bot.

Spoken: That's th' place te gan if yor matched to fite; thae'll fetch ye doon te yor wite if yor ower heavy. Thae feed ye on floor broth ivory meel en thae put it doon at th' frunt dor e' th' hoose yor livin in. Wen th' tornkee opins th' dor, put yor hand oot en yil get a ad iv a shot box we nee lid, en vary littil inside it; it's grand stuff for th' wumin foaks te paipor th' walls with. It sticks te yor ribs, but it's not muaid for a man this hes te yew coals. Bide eway if thae'll let ye.

The historic city of Durham.

THE DURHAM STRIKE

This poem was written by Tommy Armstrong at the time of the biggest coal miners strike in 1892 when the whole of Durham Coalfield was locked out. The mine owners were seeking a reduction in the miners wages and after twelve weeks, the mines were re-opened when the miners accepted a ten per cent reduction[6]. The poem, which was sold to raise funds, clearly stated where the blame lay and Tommy 'vented his spleen' at the owners in the chorus.

The last four lines of the poem are inscribed on the new headstone at Tommy's grave which was unveiled by Arthur Scargill at Tanfield in 1986.

In our Durham County, I am sorry for to say
That hunger and starvation is increasing every day;
For the want of food and coals we know not what to do,
But with your kind assistance, we will stand the struggle through.
I need not state the reason why we have been brought so low,
The masters have behaved unkind, which everyone will know;
Because we won't lie down and let them treat us as they like,
To punish us they've stopt their pits and caused the present strike.

Chorus:
May every Durham colliery owner that is in the fault,
Receive nine lashes with the rod, then be rubbed with salt.
May his back end be thick with boils, so that he cannot sit,
And never burst until the wheels go round at every pit.

The pulley wheels have ceased to move, which went so swift around.
The horses and the ponies too are brought from underground;
Our work is taken from us now, they care not if we die,
For they can eat the best of food, and drink the best when dry.
The miner, and his partner too, each morning have to roam
To seek for bread to feed the little hungry ones at home;
The flour barrel is empty now, their true and faithful friend,
Which makes the thousands wish to-day the strike was at an end.

Chorus

We have done our very best as honest working men,
To let the pits commence again we've offered to them "ten".
The offer they will not accept, they firmly do demand
Thirteen and a half per cent, or let their collieries stand.
Let them stand, or let them lie, to do with them as they choose,
To give them thirteen and a half, we ever shall refuse.
There're always willing to receive, but not inclined to give,
Very soon they won't allow a working man to live.

Chorus

With tyranny and capital they never seem content,
Unless they are endeavouring to take from us per cent;
If it was due what they request, we willingly would grant;
We know it's not, therefore we cannot give them what they want.
The miners of Northumberland we shall for ever praise,
For being so kind in helping us those tyrannising days;
We thank the other counties too, that have been doing the same.
For every man who reads will know that we are not to blame.

Hard times in Waldridge in the 1920s – Above: A soup kitchen.
Below: Scavaging for coal.

FUNNY NUAIMS IT TANFEELD PIT

This poem was written by Tommy Armstrong who was prone to using correct names of characters in his works, so there is every likelihood that those mentioned here are people he knew.

IF yil be quiet aul try te sing e vorse,
If yor nee bettor wid aw shoor yil be nee worse
It's aboot sum faimis workmin we had it oor pit,
We little picks, or bigins, that cud eethor stand or sit.

> *Chorus:*
> *Fal the dal, the day,*
> *Fal th' dal, the dido*

Th' forst thit aul menshin he stands eboot e yard,
He cums freh Caimbridge, his nuaim yiv aftin ard;
Hees is stiff eboot th' back, is th' neb iv a duck;
Sum dae he will be eeten becaws th' cawl 'im Pluck.

> *Chorus*

Th' next is e straingor, his nuaim aul not forget,
He wis catcht it Timmith, but hees geting oot th' net.
Th' Pluck is vary tuaisty, but if aw ad me wish,
Ad wid raithor eet the straingor, becaws th' cawl 'im Fish.

> *Chorus*

Th' next is e pumpor, th' moast pitmin kens,
Browt up in his cuntry, feedin' ducks en hens;
He cums te th' pit it mornens wiv his botil en his box;
Ye wid think th' hoons wis eftor 'im becaws th' cawl 'im Fox.

> *Chorus*

Th' next is e foringor, but hees nee warse for that;
His wark's alwis plaicd like th' tuthors in th' flat.
Hees quiet in sivil buaith in dae leet en dark;
Hees cum'd oot th' wattor, for his second nuaim is Shark.

> *Chorus*

Th' next is a champyin, he gans be Butchor Bob,
He once wis e butchor, but he tired iv hees gob;
He fettild beef en muttin for te fill up hungry holes,
But noo hees in th' Busty muaiking roondy coals.

Miners at East Tanfield.

So thares Bob, th' butchor, en thares Eligea Tuck;
Kaity O, Gigor O, Shagor O, en Pluck;
Th' Fox en the Fish, en thare th' monstor Shark,
Th' puttor cannot keep thim ganen wen thor aul it wark.

Chorus

It's Kaity O, en Gigor O, en Shagoros' wish
For te hev e suppor we th' Pluck en the Fish;
Thave engaged Bob, the butchor, for te cum en kill;
Ivory man it Tanfeeld cin cum en hev thorfill.

TH' GHOST THIT 'ANTED BUNTY

James Murray, known as Bunty, of Tanfield, performed with Tommy on social nights. As was his custom, he got drunk one night and was wending his way home when someone was determined to frighten him. As this poem by Tommy Armstrong shows, the experiment worked[7].

THIS is a sang thit's just cum'd oot,
Yi'll want te heer'd thor is nee doot,
So aw'll try to tell ye awl aboot
Th' ghost that 'anted Bunty.
Bunty lives not far fra here,
He's e terrible chep for drinkin' beer,
An' fra his yem he went eway,
But mony e tyme he's rooed th' day.
As he wis comin' yem that neet,
Something wite he chanced to meet
He stood en lyuke'd; he said "Aulreet-
But thoo cannit frighten Bunty."

Chorus: *Fal de rol de rol de ray*
Fal de rol de rol de ray
Fal de rol de rol de ray
The Ghost that haunted Bunty

Bunty sais: "If aw'd a gun
Aw wad knock th' doon or muaik th' run
Aw wad let th' see thoo'd not muaik fun,
Or try te frighten Bunty.
Cum oot e' th' way, an' let me past,
An dinnet muaik thawsel se fast;
Thoo think aw dinet knaw whe thoo is,
But aw ken nicely whe it is."
Th ghost then spread his airms buaith oot,
Which muaid poor Bunty shake en shoot
"Thou's a funny ghost, ther is ne doot,
But keep away fra Bunty."

    Chorus

Bunty then began to say,
"Aw wish aw'd guain th' tuther way,
Or sat an' drank anuther day –
Aw wadn't a been se frightent.
Aw've getten drunk noo mony a tyme,
But nivor did commit a crime;
Aw luv me nebors is mesel,
Th' warst e me, aw like me yell.
But O canny ghost if thoo'll let me be
Aw'll nivor mare gan on th' spree,
Aw'll alwis choose gud company
Te gan alang we Bunty."

Chorus

Bunty stooped te pick up e stuain,
He grappled aboot, but finding nuain,
He said, "O Ghost let me aluain,
An' aw'll be Teetotal Bunty.
Aw'll try to mind me awn affairs,
It neets an' mornins say me prairs;
Aw'll muaik th' bairns awl say their's
It neets, before they gan up stairs;
Aw'll try te be e different man,
Aw'll bide at yem beside wor Nan."
He turned aboot, an' off he ran,
But th' ghost ran eftor Bunty.

Chorus

He ran te he wis short e breeth,
He said, "Thor's nowt for me but deeth."
Th' ghost wis there, an' scringed his teeth
He still is wantin' Bunty.
He teuk poor Bunt up in his airm,
Just like is if he'd been a bairn;
He clashed him doon upon a stuain,
Wen he gat up th' the ghost wis guain;
He sais: "Thank God, yence mare aw's free,
He's had a nice bit fun we me;
Aw wonder whe th' ghost can be
Thit hes been eftor Bunty."

Chorus

Strite off yem poor Bunty ran,
He knock't at th' door an' shooted, "Nan,
Be is sharp is ivor thoo can,
Th' ghost's been after Bunty."
She torned th' lock an' eased th' sneck,
He flung his airms eroond hor neck,
His hair stood strite up fra his heed,
IIe sais, "Aw's nearly flaid to deed;
Lock th' door, he'll be here just noo."
"Get oot," say Nan, "it isn't true."
"Say that aguain, aw'll bring him te thoo;
For he's been eftor Bunty."

Chorus

THE HEDGEHOG PIE

This is an amusing poem written by Tommy Armstrong. Whether it is based on fact or not is unknown.

Aw'll sing ye e sang if yil paishantly wate,
Aboot e grand supper there's been it Street Gate;
To eat this grand supper thare only wis two,
But thae eat e yell hedgehog, sum baiken en coo.

There's e chep i' th' neiborood hes a smaul dog,
One day wen oot wauken, it catcht e hedgehog,
So te hev e bit fun we th' prize thit he got.
He thowt tive hees sel he wad tuaikt doon te Stott.

Wen he teukt doon te Stott thae erainged wat to dee,
We Kingey en Barbor thae alwis muaid free;
Ivory time thit thae went thae war hungry en drie,
So just fer e lark thae wad muaik them e pie.

Noo it ad te be kild befor starten te skind,
So thae took up e mell for te nock oot its wind;
Them thit wis prisint thae roard en thae laft,
Th' chep mist th' hedgehog en broake th' mell shaft.

Th' mell wis nee use, so thae teuk e sharp nife,
Detarmind to tuaik ewae progily's life;
Thae tried for te kill him two difforent ways,
So thae ad him to droond for te finish his days.

Th' landlady's sister mauid up e pie crust
We th' best e beef fat en sum dumplin dust;
She nickt it aul roond, mauid it tender en thin,
Th' yuven wis het, en she put th' pie in.

Wen th' pie wis in keuken, thare wis en aud man,
Aw'll not tell hees nuaim – ye may guest if ye can;
Th' smell e' the pie muaid him smack hees aud lip;
He sais: "If aw'd e crust aw wid try for e dip."

Barbor en Kingey sat winken thor eye,
En wishen thae only cud get a bit pie;
Thae wor watchin th' mistress esteed e' thor gill,
Th' smell wis that nice thae cud ardly keep still.

Tom th' butcher, to sute them seun fund oot e plan,
He sais : "Drink off yor gills, be is sharp is ye can;
Gan inte th' meat hoose en lae aul things bie,
En aw'll watch th' mistris en steal ye the pie."

In th' meat house thae only had been e short while,
Wen thae saw th' pie cumen thae started to smile;
Tom sais: "Get it eaten, twis fettild for Stott,
If he cums he'll gan mad," Kingey sais: "Man it's hot."

For awl it wis het, thae put up wiv its sting,
"Aw dee like e rabbit," sais Barbor te King.
Thae each had e lump e hedgehog i' thor hand,
Sais Kingey to Barbor: "By jove! but its grand."

Time thae wor on eaten, thare went in e dog,
King tos't it e buain thit belanged th' hedgehog.
Saien, "Thare's e bit rabbit" but th' dog wadint hed.
Saes Kingey: "Thoo's pawky; thoo's ower weel fed."

Te get th' pie eaten, thae buaith wired in,
Te th' gravy ran off buaith thor noses en chin;
Wen Stott shoad th' skin e th' pie thit thae'd had,
Thae luckt it each uthor, en tornd vary bad.

Sais Barbor te Kingey, "Jack aw wadin't cair,
But progils cums noo ware thor yused to be hair!
Aw bowt e 'ard hat en aw tied it tite doon,
But th' progils cum faster, en went throo th' croon."

A raiser's nee yuse – thae buaith shave wiv e saw
Like iceshogils faulen, thae drop freh thor jaw;
Barber's en trubil, Kingey far warse –
He cannot lie soon or sit doon on hees a-e.

THE KAISER AND THE WAR

The last verse of this poem indicates that the First World War was nearly over so this poem was probably written by Tommy Armstrong just before it was published in the Consett and Stanley Chronicle on the 27th September 1918.

Kaiser Bill is busy still, he tells us what he means,
By building all these floating mines and likewise submarines.
He thinks he can defeat the world and rule both land and sea,
We know what he is trying for and what he will not be.
To murder and destruction he is doing all he can,
This has been his motto ever since the war began.
His weapons are all special made, the innocent to kill,
God send the gout to both the feet of dirty Kaiser Bill.

It makes our very blood run cold each day to read the news,
The ships which they are putting down, their passengers and crews.
Not a living soul on board will they attempt to save,
They stand and laugh to see them go down to a watery grave.
They say it is their orders, that every ship they see,
Which they can, they must put down, no matter whose it be.
Whatever he tells us to do we must obey his will,
May the gout run up the legs of selfish Kaiser Bill.

To be the King of England was German Bill's ambition,
He was coming through by Belgium without asking their permission.
From there he had to fight his way until he got to France,
To England he was coming next, but did not get the chance.
"Britons never shall be slaves" we very often sing,
But we would have a German song if German Bill was King.
Instead of being on Britain's throne – he'll be put through the mill,
Then every German sausage made will taste of Kaiser Bill.

On the sea and in the sea and high up in the air,
If any murders can be done, you will find them there.
The Zeppelins do their work by night, they keep inside all day,
It suits them best when dark and late, for taking lives away.
But we have got his master now, and he has got to know,
That we can fly above the Zepps, and send them down below.
There's nothing that he can invent, the Zeppelin's place to fill,
It's nearly broke the tender heart of dirty Kaiser Bill.

He was the first to start the war, the first to cry for peace,
Since he knew it was refused – his vengeance has increased.
The war will soon be over, and the Allies will have won,
Then he will have time to sit and think of what he's done.
He has made himself a name which he will always keep,
His murders will be talked about at both sides of the deep.
May he suffer both night and day the Scriptures to fulfil,
When he is dead, the name will live – of dirty Kaiser Bill.

Burnopfield & District War Memorial.

MARLA HILL DUCKS

Imprisoned for Trespassing

Yet another funny poem written by Tommy Armstrong and which has been published in numerous places. It is still very popular and sung by various folk singers.

NOO if ye'll pae itenshin a moment or two,
Aw'll tell ye a storee aw naw te be true.
It a small collry village tha caul Marla Hill,
For te tell the suiam storee thar's men liven still.
It's aboot twenty ducks thit went oot for te play
Upon a aud pastor, one fine sumor's day;
But the farmer ispied them, en teuk them wholesale,
En fund them fresh lodgings in Marla Hill Jail.

Noo the pastor tha plaid on wis worthlis en bare,
Thor wasint a blaid a green grass growen thair;
Tha had been trespasen, en coudint deni'd,
But, like uthor prisoners, tha shud a been tried.
Wivoot judge or joory, he teuk them away,
He nivor once ax't if tha had owt to say;
If he'd geen them a chance, tha wid awl geten bail,
But he teuk them is prisnors te Marla Hill Jail.

Noo in Marla Hill prisin tha hadint been lang,
Till tha ax'd one anuther wat had tha dun rang,
Thit tha sud be captord en closely confined
In a dark dreery dungin be Marla Hill hind.
Tha nue vary weel thit tha warnit it yem,
En ta be see ill-treated tha thowt 'twis a shem;
It muaiks me sorry ta tell ye th' tale
Aboot th' young prisnors in Marla Hill Jail.

For days tha were lock'd up, buaith hungry en drie.
But to brick th' door opin tha thowt tha wid trie
We thor nebs en thor claws tha sune muaid a road throo
Wen th' hind wis it wark wi his horses and plue.
Sixteen of th' twenty got nicely away,
Tha quack'd en tha shoot'd, is much is ta sae:
"O liberty's sweet," en kept waggin' thor tail,
En that's hoo tha gat oot a Marla Hill Jail.

Thare wis still fower left in this miserable den,
Th' twenty belanged to three different men;
So tha met en tha thowt th' best way for to dae
'Twis for them ta gan doon th' Land Steward to see.
Tha went, en wis welcom'd he tret them so kind,
He laid all th' blame on the Marla Hill hind;
Wile telling thor storee th' Steward grue pale,
Wen tha told him thor ducks wis in Marla Hill Jail.

Wen leeven, the Steward to them he did say:
"Tell th' hind th' ducks must be awl set away."
Tha thowt 'twis awl reet wen th' Steward tha seed,
But th next news th' had ta pay ninepence a-heed.
Thar'll be ducks on th' pastor wen th' Steward en Hind
Is laid doon belaw, like the rest of mankind;
Tha'll be sent tiv a place for ta weep en ta wail.
Buaith th' govnor en turn-kee of Marla Hill Jail.

Marley Hill miners, circa 1900.

MURDER OF MARY DONNELLY

Jeremiah O'Connor, a widower aged 52 years, lodged with the Donnelly family in Peel Street, West Stanley. On the evening of the Monday 14th December 1908, O'Connor and ten year old Mary Donnelly were seen at

the front door of the house and shortly afterwards, in a lane nearby leading into the country. Neither of them returned to the house so search parties were arranged. On Saturday the 19th December, O'Connor was found and arrested then on the following day, the body of Mary Donnelly was found in a field of Pea Farm. She had been outraged before and after her death and her body had been cut open from below the breastbone to the lower part of her body[8].

Following a trial at Durham Assizes in February 1909, O'Connor was convicted of the murder of Mary Donnelly and sentenced to death. He was hanged in Durham Gaol on Tuesday the 23rd February 1909[9].

Mary Donnelly's memorial

The story of the murder is recorded in this poem written by Tommy Armstrong.

> While life exists and memory good, we ever shall remember,
> The cruel murder that was done on the fourteenth of December;
> A man as lodger once in West Stanley used to dwell,
> He stayed with Thomas Donnelly, a man that we know well.
>
> Donnelly had a little girl, she was but ten-year-old.
> When we think about her death, it makes our blood run cold.
> It was on a Monday night, a cruel part to play,
> This lodger left West Stanley and enticed the girl away.
>
> This loving little creature was far too young to know,
> What the man was going to do, or where she had to go.
> She was taken to a lonely place, the murderer had a knife,
> And when he had done as he choosed, he took away her life.

At nine o'clock she had not come, the mother thought her long;
At ten o' clock the father said, there must be something wrong,
The father to the mother said, go tell Inspector Stark
And I will go in search of her although the night is dark.

Inspector Stark and Officers, along with working men,
Commenced their search that evening shortly after ten.
Close upon a week was spent, searching night and day,
By scores of willing helpers, at home and far away.

Ponds were dragged both far and near for many miles around.
And Reservoirs run dry to see if the body could be found.
Whickham, Swallwell, Rowland's Gill, likewise Gibside Wood,
Was searched by officers and men without rest or food.

On the nineteenth of December, the man for which they sought,
Near Barcus Close and Tanfield by officers was caught.
They took him up to Consett, and locked him in a cell,
But how his thoughts and mind was, there's no one can tell.

The searchers still continued on, they ne' er seemed to tire,
To find the body of the child was all they did desire.
The twentieth of December which was on a Sabbath Day,
Inspector Stark with volunteers from West Stanley bent their way.

While searching near the Pea Farm, the mystery was revealed,
The body of the child was found in the corner of a field.
From the field to villages, the news was spread around.
That the body of the child that morning had been found.

NANNY'S A MAIZOR

This poem written by Tommy Armstrong, is still a favourite among folk singers in the north east of England and is often performed at concerts. However, the question arises: Was this a play on words by Tommy? Did he mean Nanny was amazing or was he referring to Nanny being a 'mazer' which is described in the Oxford English Dictionary as a 'hardwood drinking vessel'. 'Mazer' in pitmatic would certainly come out as 'Maizor' and in the poem, Nan certainly drank enough for her to be described as a 'drinking vessel'.

WOR Nan an me muaid up wor minds te gan an catch the train,
For te gan to th' toon te bie sum clais for wor little Billy an Jain;
But when we gat te Rowlinsgill th' mornen trane wis gone,
An thair wis ne mair te gan that way te fifteen minits te one.
So aw say te wor Nan, "Its a lang way te gan,"
Aw saw biv hor fuaice she was vext;
But aw sais, "Nivor mind, we heh plenty a time,
So we'll stop an gan in we th' next,"
She gav a bit smile, when aw spoak up an said:
"Thare's a public-hoose alang heer –
We'll gan alang thare an heh worsels warmd,
An a glas a th' best bittor beer."
Nan wis see stoot aw nue she cudint wauk,
An she didnt seem willin te trie;
Wen aw think a th' truble aw had wiv her that day,
If aw likt aw cud brust an crie.

Station, Rowlands Gill.

Rowlands Gill Railway Station where Tommy and Nan missed the train.

Chorus:
Ay but Nanny's a maisor, a maisor she'll remane,
Is lang is aw liv a winnit forget th' day thit we lost th' trane.

So away we went te th' publick-hoose, an wen we gat te th' dor,
She sais, "We'll gan te th' parlour end," for auve nivor been in befor,
So in we went en teuk wor seets, an before aw rung th' bell
Aw axt hor what sh' was gan te drink. "Wey," sh' sais, "th' suaim is
    thesel."
So aw called for two gills a th' best bittor beer,
She pade for thim when thae cum in;
But eftor she swalyd three-pairts iv her gill,
She sade 'Bob, man aw wid raithor hev gin'.
So aw called for a glass a th' best Holans gin,
An she gobild it up th' first trie;
Sais aw te war Nan, "Thoo's is gud is a man."
She sais, "Bob, man, aw felt very drie."
So aw called for anuthor, an that went th' suaim way;
Aw sais, "That 'ill settle thee thorst."
She sais, "Aw've had two, an aw's nee better noo
Then aw was when aw swalyd th' forst."

Chorus

She sat an drank te she gat tite; she sais "Man, aw feel vary queer."
"Wey," aw says, "thoo's had nine glasses a gin te maw three gills a
    beer."
She lows'd hor hat an then hor shawl, an tost them on te th' flor;
Aw thowt she wis gan te be rang in hor mind, so a set meesel close
    te th' dor.
She sais, "Giv is order, aw'll sing a bit sang,"
Aw sat an aw gloward at hor.
Aw thowt she wis joken for aw'd nivor heerd
Wor Nanny sing ony befor.
She gav is a tuch a "Th' Row I' th' Gutter,"
She pleesed ivory one thit wis thare;
Thar wis neebody in but wor Nanny an me,
An aw laft te me belly wis sair.
She tried te stand up for te sing "Th' Cat Pie,"
But she fell doon an muiad such a clattor.
She smasht fower chairs an th' landlord com in,
An he said, "What th' deuce is th' mattor?"

Chorus

Th' landlord sais, "Is this yor wife, an whare de yea belang?"
Aw sais, "It is, an she's teun a fit wi' trien te sing a bit sang."
He flung his airms around hor waist an traild hor across th' flor,
An Nan, poor sowl, like a dorty hoose cat, wis tumild ootside a th' dor.
Thar she wis lyen, buaith groanen en crien,
Te clame hor aw reely thowt shem;
Aw tried for te lift hor, but aw cudint shift hor.
Aw wisht aw had Nanny at yem.
Th' paipor man said he wid give hor a ride,
So we lifted hor inte th' trap;
She wis that tite she cudint sit up,
So we fasind hor doon wiv e strap.
She cudint sit up, and she wadint lie doon,
She kickt till she broak th' convains;
She lost a nue baskit, hor hat, an hor shawl
That mornen, throo lossen th' tranes.

Chorus

The Towneley Arms, Rowlands Gill where Tommy wrote the poem
'Nanny's a Maizor'. This is now a very nice block of apartments called
Towneley House.

TH' NUE RALEWAE TE ANFEELD PLANE

The people who lived in the district embracing Annfield Plain, West Stanley, Tanfield Lea and surrounding areas had long complained about the absence of railway facilities. Their complaints and patience were eventually rewarded when the North Eastern Railway Company built a railway line from Newcastle to Annfield Plain. It opened at the end of 1893 but to carry goods only, then at the beginning of 1894, passenger trains started running[10]. This poem was written by Tommy Armstrong to commemorate the event.

Annfield Plain Railway Station.

It wis in the month e Novembor, en ipon th' thorteenth dae,
Th' eer in hiteen ninety three, wen th' nue ralewae
Wis oapind oot for minoril, for th' cumpiny wis flade
Te trust th' lives e wor cany aud wives, th' line been nuely lade.

Spoken: It wis vary thowtfil e th' ralewae cumpiny te trie th' line we deed stock forst, but thor wid nivor been e ralewae muaid tiv Anfeeld Plane if it hadint been for Billy Bulmor, Ridily, th' owerseeor, en Bil Indyan, West Stanla, en th' oanly wae thit we cin recompense thim is we singen th' chorus -

Chorus:
We'll sing in praise e Billy Bulmor, Ridily en Indyan th' suaim,
We shud trie it th' next big elechshin te put M.P. te thor nuaim,
It thor awn expense for th' cuntry-side thae laibor'd neet en dae,
Lang mae th' liv for te ride up en doon ipin th' nue ralewae.

Wen hiteen ninety fower cum in, the tauk wis neet en dae,
Wunderen wen the tranes wid start ipon th' nue ralewae.
Genuairy past en went, en eesed es e wor pane,
Febuairy th' forst com in, en browt es th' mornen trane.

Spoken: Ye shud seen th' cany aud wives gigin eboot, sum we th' glass
e thor hand – hauf tite, drinken e helth te th' nue ralewae. Tripey Nan
shoots: join we me en we'll sing –

Chorus

Mony e scor freh Stanla went, likewis freh Tanfeeld Lee,
En met it Sheel Raw staishin, th' mornen trane te see.
Wen thare ard th' wussill blaw it set th' plaice elive,
Three cheers went up freh yung en aud, wen th' forst trane did erive.

Spoken: Aw wis stanen beside a chep wen th' shooten started, aul
nivor forget it, he vary neer shifted my nolidge box off its plaice, he
had hes mooth wide oapen, it just put e th' mind iv e empy hoose, he
had nee teeth in, aw cud see reet doon hes throate en neerly throo th'
back dor, but aw shifted me stand en began te sing –

Chorus

There wis mony a score got in te ride te Annfeeld Plane,
Just te sae thaid ad e ride, in th' forst nue ralewae trane.
Two cany awd fish wives, like the rest th' sade thaid geten thor wish,
Thae wid oftin be oot e th' cuntry noo we thor baskets en thor fish.

Spoken: Jack Smith had e gam cock clocken, en he wis doon it Bob
Johnstin's it Sheel Raw, geten e clecken e weel bred eggs, he ad six e
one pockit en sivin e the turthor, but wen he got tiv Anfeeld Plane he
oanly ad two, the carrigis war that full his eggs wis awl broken, when
he gat yem he put he's cote under the clocker, he still expects te git th'
breed, aw wish he may, aw left im thare singen –

Chorus

If ye want te gan te th' peopil's paliss, Or th' Nuegit Street Impire,
Ye heh nee caul te bothor yor heed, e cab or e trap te hire.
Th' tranes is runen for te sute es awl ipon th' Sheel Raw line,
Ye can gan e th' mornen or the eftorneun, for te see th' pantomime –

Chorus

OAKEY'S KEEKER

Joseph Elliott was the 'Keeker' (Surface Foreman) at Oakey's Colliery about whom Tommy Armstrong wrote this poem. It must have been written during the early part of 1878 because on the 28th February that year, Joseph Elliott appeared before the Magistrates at Lanchester Petty Sessions seeking their advice. He wanted to know if he could prosecute the author of the poem for 'libel and scandal'. Full details of the proceedings are contained in the Chapter 7: CONTROVERSIES.

O OAKEYS! O Oakeys! what makes you so bad?
It's enough for to make all your workmen go mad;
We should like very well to know what you mean,
The way you go on from the pit to the screen.
You treat us coal hewers just as you think fit,
The wages are small that are paid in the pit;
But what we are making we really don't know,
Since they have sent us Old Maiden Law Joe.

This famous old keeker must not understand
How we are tormented with ramble and band;
The ramble comes down, after firing a shot.
Among the loose coals, and it cannot be got.
By the light of a candle it cannot be found –
Daylight is different from being underground.
If this old keeker would only think so,
We would speak better of Old Maiden Law Joe.

To do his duty is nothing but right,
But in hurting coal hewers he takes a delight;
If he pleases the masters that's all he cares for,
Suppose that he hungers poor men to the door.
At half-past six in the morning he starts
To fill up the box, which is only two quarts;
If he gets the first tub, how pleased he will go
And say, "That's a start for Old Maiden Law Joe."

He was at the Bank-foot – that's near to the Plain –
We wish he was only back there again.
While he was there he was doing the same –
He must have been born without feeling or shame.
They say there's a medium in every case,
He's not a fit man to have such a place;
For he has no feeling for men that's below
This hairy-faced rascal – Old Maiden Law Joe.

This Maiden Law tyrant does nothing but shout,
"Who belongs to this tub? because it's laid out;"
He smacks his old lips, his old hands he will rub,
Because he has taken a poor man's tub.
Amongst the coal hewers how well he is known,
His hardness towards them he always has shown;
What makes him do it I really don't know –
This cruel imposter, Old Maiden Law Joe.

I hope all the screeners, as well as old Joe,
Will think of the men that are working below.
Perhaps in a pit they may never have been –
There's where the hardship may daily be seen.
How would they like it, if they knew what you made,
When the pay came and the money not paid?
I hope that the whiskers so quickly will grow,
As to fill up the mouth of Old Maiden Law Joe,

Now, Joey Badun, you silly old man!
You have nearly done all the ill that you can;
With age your whiskers are quite turning grey,
I think it is time you were starting to pray.
I never did like to wish anyone harm,
But I doubt you will go to a place where it's warm.
It's nothing but right to reap what you sow –
They'll burn your whiskers, Old Maiden Law Joe.

Now if you take ill and be confined to your bed.
Do you think your masters will keep you with bread?
Do you think your masters will visit you then,
For all you have always imposed on the men?
For all you did for them their money to save,
If you were dead, would they go to your grave?
Not one single step with your corpse will they go –
Because it's that rascal, Old Maiden Law Joe.

Now, Mr Badun, I'm writing too long,
I hope you'll forgive if there's anything wrong.
When God calls upon you, what will you say?
Those tubs will be standing before you that day.
If the old Devil sees you, he'll give a great shout
"That's Oakey's old keeker who laid the tubs out."
God will then say, "Down to hell you must go,
If you are the keeker called Maiden Law Joe."

OAKEY'S STRIKE

This poem was written by Tommy Armstrong in the Black Horse Public House, Red Row, Beamish in 1885. William McGuire, who boasted about his prowess as a poet had moved to Tanfield for work. Armstrong and Maguire were great rivals so a contest between them was arranged. Many miners who had gathered, were to choose the subject and decided upon the evictions of miners from their homes during the recent strike at Oakey's Pit[11]. Maguire's song has been forgotten but Tommy's became famous and is still popular today.

The Black Horse Public House, Red Row, Beamish where the contest was held.

IT wis in November en aw nivor will forget
Th' polisses en th' candymen it Oakey's hooses met;
Johny, th' bellmin, he wis thare, squinten roond eboot;
En he plaic'd three men it ivory hoose te torn th' pitmen oot.

    Chorus:
Oh wat wad aw dee if ad th' poower me sel,
Aw wid hang th' twenty candymen en Johny thit carry's th' bell.

Thare th' went freh hoose to hoose te put things on th' road,
But mind th' didnt' hort thorsels we liften hevy loads;
Sum wid carry th' poker oot, th' fendor, or th' rake,
If th' lifted two it once is wis a greet mistake.

    Chorus

Sum e theese dandy-candy men wis drest up like e cloon;
Sum ad hats wivoot e flipe, en sum wivoot e croon;
Sum ad nee laps ipon thor cotes but thare wis one chep warse;
Ivory time he ad te stoop it was e laffible farse.

    Chorus

Thare wis one chep ad nee sleeves nor buttins ipon hees cote;
Enuthor ad e bairns hippin lapt eroond his throte.
One chep wore e pair e breeks thit belang tiv e boi,
One leg wis e sort iv e tweed, th' tuthor wis cordyroi.

Chorus

Next thare cums th' maistor's, aw think thae shud think shem
Depriven wives en familys of a comfortible yem.
But wen thae shift freh ware thae liv, aw hope thail gan te hell,
Elang we th' twenty candy men, en Johny thit carry's th' bell.

Chorus

Oakey's Cottages.

OLD FOLKS TEA AT WEST STANLEY

This poem, written by Tommy Armstrong, first appeared in the Consett Chronicle in 1912 in appreciation of a wonderful tea provided in West Stanley Store for old people living in the area. It describes the food and the service provided by the Working Men's Clubs. The first verse gives the date of the event as the thirteenth of July[12]. With a variation to the fourth verse, the poem again appeared in the local newspaper in 1918 when Tommy gave the date of the event as the 27th July[13].

I've been at grand suppors, grand dinnors and teas;
In chapels and churches, likewise in marquees;
Enjoyment and pleasure I always could find
If the company I met with were lively inclined;
I've had some grand treats in the days that's gone by,
But I went to a tea, the thirteenth of July;
I never saw such a grant set-out before,
Like the Old people's Treat at West Stanley Store.

Seven hundred old people, all hearty and gay,
Some were bald-headed, while others were grey;
With sticks and with crutches, 'twas grand for to see
The way that they hobbled upstairs to the tea.
On entering the hall where the tables were set,
The sight which I saw I shall never forget;
People from sixty to eighty, and more,
Were all at the tea in West Stanley Store.

Whitebread, well buttered, and brown bread the same,
And many more spices than what I can name;
There was teacakes and custard, seed bread and rice,
Tarts made of apples, biscuits and spice.
There was all kinds of jellies and blackcurrant jam,
Beef, tongue and mutton, pickles and ham;
Tomatoes, bananas, was there in galore
At the Old People's Tea in West Stanley Store.

I would like to have mentioned each working man's name,
But to mention the Clubs will perhaps do the same;
There's the 'West Stanley Workmen's' and 'East Stanley' too,
The 'Excelsior' and 'Norman', and 'Empire' true;
The 'Central', 'Oxhill', and the 'Social', South Moor,
The 'Union', 'Victoria' and the 'Pioneer' sure;
Are working together as they have done before,
For the Old People's Tea in West Stanley Store

(Version of the fourth verse in 1918.)
The Working Men's Clubs are the old people's friend,
The members don't care what they give or they spend.
The names of the clubs I am not very sure,
But there's one at East Stanley and one at South Moor.
The West Stanley Workmen's and the Central Oxhill,
The Garden House Club and the Empire still,
Are working together, as they have done before,
For the Old People's Treat at West Stanley Store.

The Old People's Treat has been on seven year,
It is not provided by the brewers of beer,
All is provided by Workingmen's Clubs,
There's not much to get from the owners of pubs.
Those owners have men to look after each bar,
While writing, it is not to them I refer;
For, like other workmen, they just have a wage,
Paid by the owners, who do them engage.

Thanks to each steward, each stewardess as well,
The good they have done there's no one can tell;
Likewise the committees and members the same,
For helping old people, they've made a good name.
The waiters, God bless them, we should not forget
The way the old people was cared for and treat;
If we live till next year, I will meet you once more
At the Old People's Tea in West Stanley Store.

West Stanley Co-operative Society.

A POAM TO THE KAISER

On the 29th December 1916, The Consett & Stanley Chronicle published the following letter and poem from Tommy. The first two sentences of the letter relate to the year 1902 when Tommy had made a temporary move to Whitley Bay and started a business as a newsagent.

CHRISTMAS WORD FROM OUR OLD FRIEND
THE TANFIELD POET

Mister Edietor, – Sir, aw wis just thinking aboot ye th tuther dea. It's fowerteen eeer since yee en me met et Whitley Bae. Mind there's been i lot e changes since then me man. Iverything es add ther change an yor awd frin Tommy es add his change like other things aroond us. Aw's nowt like the siam chep noo thit aw was th last time we ad e bit crack, en if iver we meet eguain yil see e greet change in me. Ye shud see me swanking up an doon the Frunt street it Stanley throo th week. When the street isin't see thang aw wear e stick in one hand en gluve on th tuthor – e proper swell. Aw dorsent ventor up th frunt on e Setorday for feer aw nock sum body throo e shop window, so aw gan up th back wae.

A met e chep beside th Commercial Hotel th tuther dae aw adinit seen for fivteen eer. He waakt past me en aw did th siam wi' im. Wi didint ken each uther. When he got e few yords ewae he turned aroond en shooted it th top iv is voyce "Is that Tommy Airmstrang?" Aw teld him it wes. If aw adin't teld im sum body elce wad. E sais "Noo hes th been wounded it th frunt Tommy?" Aw sais "No aws woanded aul e one side. Reet frae me toes end te th sentor of me Nolidge Box." He sade e was sorrie to see me in th wae aw wes; aw believed him. He said "We'l hev e drink for auld lang sine." He wis sorprised when I said aw wes teatotil, in so aw wes befor we pairted. An before we pairted he put a ten shillin note in te me hand. There's lots like him Mister Edidditor aw wish te tell ye how I'm getting invitations frae th Biggins ove our land te spend ma Xmas and New Eer wi them. Aw nivver thowt aw wis see weil naun emang th arostroacey. Only this week ave ed a letter frae our new Prime Minster Mr Loyed George. E wants me ta gan en ha ma Dinner wiv em on New Ers dae. Aw mite gan, aw'l see. Aw had enuther letter last week on Tuesday neet frae a gentleman at Wauker ta dine wi im on Xmas dae. Aw divint ken im. It's not es far es London so aw think awl gan te Wauker,

Prime Minister David Lloyd George.

The Kaiser.

but believe me aul not gan to wauk hor wey. No, aul gan we th buss, ald get thare sharper.

God Bless us, heir's th Postman aguain; aw wish he wid caul next door aw hevint five minits peace. It wis e letter frae th Kaiser. Hes a chep ave niver seen but ave ard en red plenty eboot im, aw once ard ma grandfether sae when he wis in Germiny im en th Kaiser's fether swapt dogs. Aw heve nowt te dee wi that awve sent im en answer.

A POAM TO THE KAISER

Kaiser Bill from Germiny why do you write to me?
I think you are the only man I do not want to see;
There never would have been a war ad it not been for you;
You thought to rule the world by now, that's what you'll never do.

You are the most unfeeling man that ever lived on earth,
If you should die a sudden death 'tis more than you are worth.
God's name you've oft times mentioned up to the present times,
You should bear in mind that "God above does not believe in Crime."

You say that God is merciful, in Him you put your trust,
But if you do not win this war, you'll say He is not just.
You now should ask for pardon for the crimes which you have done,
Because you know this awfull war by you will not be won.

Pray God to take you in His Hands and guide you safely through,
For when you know you cannot win you'll see what He will do.
Your days on earth are numbered; you need not seek for peace,
I hope before this year is out your troubles will increase.

For what you've done to children, their fathers and their mothers
You tortured them most shamefully and many, many others.
Little babies six months old torn from their mother's breasts
The mothers treat with cruelty, taken and undressed,
And then so cruelly murdered by those dirty Huns,
You thought they had done clever with their bayonets and their guns.

TH' ROW BETWEEN TH' CAIGES

Tommy Armstrong wrote this poem in 1908 when according to legend, he went to work in a bad mood having had an argument with the overseer. A newly constructed lift-cage had been installed to operate alongside the old one. Tommy's feelings towards the overseer led him to think how the old cage must feel towards the new cage. He imagined a fight arising between the two cages and that day, he composed this poem[14].

Two miners crouch in this cage.

ONE mornen wen aw went ta wark, th' seet wis most exsiten,
Ad ard a noise, en luckt eroond, en we de ye think wis fiten ?
Aw stud amais'd en at thim gaisd, te see thim in such raiges;
For aw nivor seed e row like that between th' Brockwil caiges.

Wor aud caig sais, "Cum over th' gaits, becaws it's mei intenshin
Te let th' see wethor thoo or me is th' best invenshin."
The' neuin been rais'd, teuk off his clais, then at it thae went dabin ;
Th' blud wis runen doon th' skeets, en past th' weimin's cabin.

Wor aud caige sais, "Let's heh me clais, thoo thowt thit thoo cud
    flae me;
But if aw'd been is young is thoo aw's certain aw cud pae th'".
Th' paitint nockt hees ankel off, en th' buaith ad cutten fuaices;
Th' shifters rapt three for te ride, so th' buaith went to thor plaices.

Wen ganen up en doon th' shaft, th' patint caige did threetin
for te tuaik wor audin's life if thae stopt it meeten;
Wor aud cage bauld oot is thae pas't; "Thoo nasty, dorty paitint,
Rub thee ies eguain th' skeets – aw think thoo's ardly wakinit."

Th' paitint te wor aud caige sais; "Altho' aw be e strangor,
Aw kin work me wark is weel is thoo, an free th' men freh daingor:
Noo, if th' rope shud brick we me, aud skinny jaws, just watch us,
Thoo'l see me clag on te th' skeets, for aw's full e springs en catches."

Wor aud caige te th' paitint sais; "Aw warnd thoo think thoo's clivor.
Becaws thi'v polished thoo we paint, but thoo'l not last for ivor;
Th' paint on thoo 'ill weer awae, en then thoo's lost thei beuty;
Th' nivor painted me at awl, en still aw've deun me deuty."

Th' braiksmin browt thim buaith te bank, th' mischeef for te settil;
Thae fit freh five o'clock te six, en th' paitint won th' battle.
It teuk th' braiksmin half e shift te clag thim up we plaistors;
Wor aud caige sent hees noatece in, but just te vext th' maistors.

Spoken: Thor matcht to fite eguain, but not under Queensbury Rools.
Wor aud caige fancies fiten we th' bare fist. Aw'll let ye naw wen it
comes off. It 'ill heh to be kept quiet; if the bobby gets to naw, thae'll
be buaith teun, becaws th' winit aloo bare fist fitein noo. Keep lucken
in th' Christian Arald, en yil see wen it comes off, en ware. Thor's six
to fower on the auden noo. Bet nowt te that dae, en aw'll see ye in the
field; it's a cheet.

A lift cage with miners at a coal mine.

TH' ROW I' TH' GUTTER

In some streets, there were open channels which had to be cleaned out and there were often rows amongst the women over the cleaning[15]. Tommy Armstrong enjoyed listening to their rantings which gave him ammunition for verse, resulting in this poem. As Tommy often used the real names of people in his works, the possibility is that those mentioned in this poem, are people he knew.

ONE day wen oot wauken aw hard sum foaks tauken,
We voices is lood is th' one o'clock gun;
For awl aw cud heer thim, aw cudint get neer thim.
For scors iv awl kinds wis injoyin th' fun.
Wiv pruven en fenden en borren en lenden,
Aw axt i' yung woman wat awl th' row meend;
Up spoak Mistris Ruttor: "It's just this awd guttor.
Thor's a row ivory day wen it hes te be cleend."

Spoken: Yis; aw spent en oor an' a half very canny. Skin and hair wis fleein an' any amaunt e secrits. If aw kin get te naw the next day it hes te be cleend aw'll be thare seun eneuf. Aw got te naw thor nick nuaims, and whe thae'n been ower kind with; en wen aw saw thim on boxin', aw sed to masel –

Chorus
Wat need we care aboot Afghans or Zulus,
Let Rushians or Prushians cum neer if thae dar;
Wi' brum en wi bussoms we'll slay thim be dussons,
Th' petticote ridgmint's the boys for th' war.

Sais young Meggy Robson tiv aud Nanny Dobson:
"Aw lent ye sum buttor a fortnith th' day;
Then ye gat a shillen, ye drunken aud villan,
Ye promist te cum en pait't back it th' pay."
"Buaith ye en th' guttor, yor shillen en butter."
Sais aud Nanny Dobson, "kin gan te th' toon;
For yor clais en Jimey's, yor bedgoons en shimees,
Is awl up th' spoot, en thae'll nivor cum doon."

Spoken: She wis lit up thare aguain. War wis on e two difforint places. Thore wis nee big guns, but thore wis sum vary big tongues; en thor neeves wis fleein, so aw torned roond to Jack Scott en aw sais –

Chorus

Young Meggy Robson feld aud Nanny Dobson,
For sayin thit hor clais en' thare Jim's wis in paun;
Then young Janey Dixon en Margit Jane Nixon
Buaith seis'd ipon Meggy for striken et Nan.
Aud Mistris Stoker com oot wi' the poker,
As seun as she saw there wis two upon Meg;
Bein' in such a spluttor she fell i' th' guttor,
En happind te brick th' sma' buain iv her leg.

Spoken: Poor aud body! It wis a bad job for hor; but it wis a gud job
for th' tuthors. She says te this day if she hadint broke hor leg she wud
heh broken sum e thor necks. So wen we heh such gud sowljors as
these –

Chorus

Wile in the bother they feld one anuther,
'Twis awful te stand en te lisson thor cries;
Aud Sally Cairns went yem tiv hor bairns,
She grapil'd the way, wi' two bonny black eyes.
Thim for to friten, en stop awl thor fiten,
The Sergint seez'd two for te tuaik them to jail;
But they iviryone seez'd him-bie gum! hoo they squeez'd him –
He off, en they cudint lay salt tiv his tail.

Spoken: Wen he gat yem he had nee hat on, nee buttons on his cote,
en three-parts ov his cote lap rovin off; en as mony scratches on his
fyece as if thord' been a undrid cats at him. Wen he wis tellin' the wife
where he'd been, she borst oot laffin, en started to sing –

Chorus

Aud Polly Trumil struck young Besse Humil,
Becaws she had cauld her a dorty nick nuaim;
They ivory one at it, they fit en they bat it,
Till not one amang thim wis fit te wauk yem.
They sent for the doctor – his nuaim wis John Proctor
An' then for the pollisses – Jacksin en Jones;
An' they sent a letter for Hall, the bonesetter,
An' it teuk him three days for te set awl the bones.

Spoken: The Battle O' Waterloo wis nowt te this one. There wis any
amount o' black eyes en broken bones. But for noses – they war awl
shapes; sum wis braid reet te one side, en sum wis braid at flat as a
pen-kyek; en as much skin en hair lyen aboot as wad muaik a hundred
shinons. So we gathered up the war gear en started te sing –

Chorus

SHEEL RAW FLUD

In November 1875 there was a weekend of terrible storms with gale force winds and floods affecting many parts of the country, particularly the north east. Two ships were wrecked on the north coast, the River Wear overflowed its banks in various places resulting in part of Chester-le-Street being submerged[16]. Tommy Armstrong wrote this poem about how the floods affected some people at Shield Row.

S'lang as aw live awl nivor forget
One Setorday wen it was se wet,
Ivory body wis nearly bet
Fra th' Setorday till th' Sunda' O!
The ducks did quack an' th' cocks did craw
For wat wis up thae diddent naw,
It nearly drooned awl Sheel Raw,
That nasty Sunda' mornin', O!

Mall Jonson tiv hor husbind sais:
"Reech me ma stockens en ma stais.
For God's suaik let me heh ma clais
Or else aw will be droonded, O!"
"Tha clais," said he, "thor guain we mine,
Like Boyd an' Elliott, up the Tyne;
Aw've leukt fra five, an' noo its nine,
This nasty Sunda' mornin' O!"

Flooding is still a danger today. Here is the flood at South Church, Bishop Auckland in 1999.

On the bed she began to rowl,
An' flung hor airms aroond th' powl,
Sa'en "Lord heh marcy on maw sowl
This nasty Sunda' mornin' O!"
Th' vary cats thae ran up staires,
Gat on thor nees ta sae thor prairs,
Thinkin thae wor gon for fairs
That nasty Sunda' mornin', O!"

Aw wis sorry for Sally Clark,
Th' fire wis oot, an' awl wis dark,
She gat oot i' bed wi' nowt but hor sark,
That nasty Sunda' mornin', O!
She muaid a splash we sich a clatter.
Thit Bob cried oot, "Sal, wat's th' mattor"
She sais, "Aw's up to me eyes i' wattor,
It must be a nasty mornin', O!"

Bob jump'd oot of he's bed an' awl,
He went where ivor he heerd hor squal,
But th' wattor wis alwis shiften Sal,
That nasty Sunda' mornin', O!"
At last th' wattor burst opin th' dor,
An' weshed away buaith Bob an' hor,
At Tinmith they wer wesh't ashore,
That nasty Sunda' mornin' O!

Shield Row Railway Station.

TH' SKEUL BORD MAN

This 'playlet' was written by Tommy Armstrong and could have been prompted by his own experiences when his daughter did not attend school in May 1900. The circumstances of the incident are contained in 'Chapter 1: WHO WAS TOMMY'.

ONE morning it haulf-past hite, aw sade te maw bit bairn,
"On we thee clais, en get off te skeul, for thoo naws thit aw want th' te lairn.
Boy: Th' skeul gans in it nine, en ye naw ifs not vary far.
Man: Thoo naws aw like for te see th' be in time, so thee beuk en thee slate's e th' drawer.

Spoken: Man: Get off te skeul is sharp is ivor thoo can.
Boy: Aw can't gan this mornen.
Man: Thoo cannot gan this mornen! wat's th' mattor we th'?
Boy: Aw heh th' tic.
Man: Thor's alwis somthing th' mattor we th' wen thoo hes te gan te skeul; if thoo dissent gan aw'll be getten e lump of paipor, en it th' boddom thare'll be ritten on –

Chorus:
Send your bairns te skeul, lairn thim aul ye can;
Scholarship is e faithful friend, en yil nivor see th' Skeul Bord man.

Boy: Aw've been vary bad for e week.
Man: Wei, aw thowt thoo'd getten th' torn;
En if aw let thee bide et yem th' dae.
Boy: Wei, aw'll trie for te gan th' morn.
Man: If thoo bides it yem th' dae, th' morn aw'll muaik thee gan,
For thoo naws vary weel th' next thing we'll get, is e summons freh th' Skeul Bord man.

Spoken: Hees Uncil Jack gat e summons th' tuthor day, but th' canny aud Judge set im cleer eftor he pade sivin-en-sixpence; en he told im if he didn't send hees bairns te skeul, en wis browt te Lanchestor eguain, he wid get hees sivin-en-sixpence back – mebee. So wen he com away he wis singen –

Chorus

So it apint that very dae.
Boy: Wen aw wis plain it th' dor.
Man: Thare wis e man, wiv e buek iv hees hand, thit aw nivor seed befor;
So aw kindly invited im in, en te tauk he seun began;
Aw suen gat te naw, be th' soond iv hees jaw, thit he wis th' Skeul Bord man.

A class of lads pose for the camera.

Spoken: He nockt it th' dor. Aw shoots, "Cum in." In he cums, he sis, "Gud mornen, Mistor Airmstrang." Aw said, "Hould on, thoo's getten te th' rang hoose." But he wadint be stopt; he sais, "Hoo mony children heh thoo got?" Aw sais, "Man, that's en impitint question." He sais, "Well, but you know what I mean; I mean how many have you had?" Aw sais, "Be oot e this, or aw'll vacsinate th'." So he tornd te wor Bess, en sais, "What family have you had." She sais, "We've ad two deed en three elive: if thae'd aul been liven, that wid be five. Is th' setesfied noo?" He nivor sade enothur word tiv he gat ootside, en he put hees fuaice eguain th' window en sais –

Chorus

Man: Wen aw axt im te sit doon – "No aw've got nee time to spare;
Aw've been at skeul en lookt throu th' books.
Boy: En aw warnd thor's e lot not thare.
Man: Ye can tuaik maw word freh th' dae, te skeul he'll hey to gan.
Boy: Aw shoar aw will, for aw's flade te deed wen aw meet we th'
Skeul Bord man.

Spoken: He hes awl th' bairns e th' cuntry side flade te deed, en not only th' bairns but thor fethors en muthors disint care eboot seein im. He sent poor Billy Potts e summons th' tuthor week for thair little Bob bein off skeul haulf e shift, en fined im five shillen en costs. Hee's been off hees meet ivor since, en that's e bad job, for im, for th' mare he eats th' mare checks he gets. Aw met im th' tuthor dae; aw wis sorry for him, awl he cu sae wis –

Man: Noo, aw want th' te gan te skeul.
Boy: Yis en aw alwis gan.
Man: Aw want th' te be a bettor scolar than me – that is if aw possibly can.
Boy: If ye hadint e plade th' troon wen like me ye wair yung;
Ye wid muaid bettor sangs, en poatry tee, en yor sangs wid e been bettor sung.

Spoken: Aw sae, wat memory's bairns hes! Thor wis en aud skeul-mate e mine com inte wor hoose one dae next week, wen aw wasint in, en we gat on e tauken aboot plaen th' troon e wor yung daes. Aw nivor noatessed im being in, becaws he wis oot it th' time. But shoor enuf aw wis e bad scholar. Aw once put buaith stockens on te one leg, en eftor that aw went to th' neet skeul three weeks throo th' dae, tiv aw wis muaid perfect; en noo aw kin read a publick-hoose sine is weel is onybody, en gan in en stop in lang is onybody; en aw think it's maw duty, since aw've fund see much gud freh educaisoon, te tell ye thit hes bairns for te –

Chorus

A woodwork class in a County Durham School.

SOOTH MEDOMSLEY STRIKE

Tommy Armstrong wrote this poem about another strike which was brought about by colliery owners seeking a reduction in the wages of the miners. The strike started at the end of 1885 and continued well into 1886. On the 2nd March 1886, twelve more miners with their wives and families were forcibly evicted from their homes at South Medomsley Colliery. They were evicted by the candymen who were guarded by a strong force of about eighty policemen. At the time of the eviction, the weather was atrocious with snow waist deep[17].

In circumstances such as these, the families and furniture were accommodated at the homes of friends until such time as the menfolk were re-employed and allocated a house by the colliery owner.

As he did in the poem about 'OAKEY'S STRIKE', Tommy lambasted the candymen who helped to evict the miners from their homes. Candymen were scrap metal dealers or rag & bone men who got their name from giving children sweets in exchange for clothes.

This particular ballad of Tommy's is still held in high regard and often sung by folk singers of today.

IF yor inclined te heer e sang aul sing e vorse or two,
En wen aws deun yil goin en sae thit ivory word is troo.
Th' miners of Sooth Medomslev thae nivor will forget
Fisick en hees tyrany, en hoo thae ad been tret;
For in th' midst iv daingor, theese ardy sons did toil,
For te earn thair daily bred see far beneeth th' soil.
Te muaik en honist livelyhood each miner did contrive,
But ye shil heer hoo thae wer sarvd in hiteen-hiety five.

Chorus
Th' miners it Sooth Medomsley thor gan te muaik sum stew,
Thor gan te boil fat Postick en his dorty candy croo.
Th' maistors shud hev nowt but soop is lang is thare elive,
In memory of thor dorty tricks in hiteen hiety five.

Belaw th' county avorage then th' men wis ten por cent.
Yit Fisick the unfeelen cor he cudint rest content
E ten por cent redushin freh th' men he did demand,
But such e strong request is this th' miners could not stand.
Th' notices wis aul sarved oot en when thae ad expired,
Aul th' geer wis browt te bank th' final shot wis fired
Te hort hees honist workmen this law lived man did strive,
He'l oftin roo for wat he did in hiteen hiety five.

Chorus

Fisick wis detarmind still mor tyrany te show,
For te get sum candy men he wandord to en fro.
He muaid hees wae te Consitt en, he sau Postick, th' bum,
He nue he liket such dorty gobs, en he wis shoor te cum.
Fisick teld im wat te dee, ware te gan en wen,
So at th' time ipointid, Postick landed wiv hees men.
We polises en candy men, th' plaice wis aul elive.
Aul throo th' strike thit Fisick caws'd in hiteen heity five.

Chorus

Commander Postick gav th' word, thae started we thor wark,
But thae wor deun it five eclock, thae dorsint stop te dark.
En wen thae ad deun aul thae cud en finish'd for the dae
Th' bobies guarded Postick en his dorty dogs awae.
Fisick wis e tyrant en th' ownors wis th' suaim
For th' torn oot th' strike tha ware th' men to blame.
Neethor them nor Postick need expect thail ivor thrive
For wat thae did te Dipton men in hiteen hiety five.

Chorus

South Medomsley Colliery.

STANLA MARKIT

This is a very funny poem written by Tommy Armstrong about his nearest market at Stanley. It is still very popular with folk singers.

IF ye be bad en off yor meat
En wid like te be put reet
Tuaik e wauk sum Fridae neet
Up te Stanla Markit.
Aul kines e doctors thare yil see,
Thor aul is buisy is cin be;
Its we te tell th' bigest lee,
While tellin ower wat thae cin dee.
Te heer thim on thae ar that clivor
Thae Gin muaik nue lungs en liver
En fact thail muaik ye liv for ivor
Up it Stanla Markit.

    Chorus:
Fol de rol de rol de ray
Fol de rol de rol de ray
Fol de rol de rol de ray
Up it Stanla Markit

Thare thail stand en guap en shoot,
En wen th' crood get roond eboot
Thae tell ye thae cin cure th' goot
Up it Stanla Markit.
Thae preech ewae en nivor smyles,
Its reely grand te see thor stiles;
Thae tell ye thae cin cure th' piles,
Turners, ulsord throtes, or biles.
Thare thail stand freh six te ten
En tell th' good thiv deun for men;
Thae think th' pitmin disent ken
Thit gans te Stanla Markit.

    Chorus

En when ye get mixt up e th' thrang
Yil find it ard te travil elang;
En yil heer sum stranger singen a sang
Up it Stanla Markit.
Thares e chep we second handed clais,
And beuts en shoos hees full e praise;
But tuaik nee noatis wat he sais
He onaly wants yor bits e pais.
Thares sasage, ducks, en savilois,
En thares e stall we nowt but tois
Te plees th' little girls en bois
Up it Stanla Markit.

Chorus

Thares bulits en spices en pies en wigs,
Taity chopers, braiks, en gigs,
En yil oftin see e chep we pigs
Up it Stanla Markit.
Thares black pudings, neerly wite,
Thor muaid te suit yor appetite;
One il sarv freh six tiv hite
Thae suit e chep thits rithor tite.
In rain or snaw ye needn't fret
Thares umborelas for ye te get
Te keep ye drie emang th' wet
Up it Stanla Markit.

Chorus

Thare yil see a grand Masheen,
It shines like silver, nice en cleen ;
It tries th' narves, e fat en leen,
Up it Stanla Markit.
Thares leg e pork, fra Rotterdam,
Baicon, beef en home-fed ham;
Black corant, en strawbary gam,
En ony emoont e veel en lam.
Ye cin get e tip, but dinit hed
If ye dinit naw hoo th' horse is bred;
Thares pots to stand belaw th' bed
Up it Stanla Markit.

Chorus

Station Road, Stanley.

TANFEELD LEE SILVOR MODIL BAND

This poem was written by Tommy Armstrong to celebrate the formation of the band in the village where he lived. In the poem, Tommy expressed appreciation to Mister Joicey, the owner of Tanfield Lea Colliery, who contributed towards the band. This was in contrast to the lambasting he used to give the colliery owners at times of strikes and lock-outs.

AW canit tell hoo glad aw is te goin we ye th' neet
For te help wor fella working men we think its nowt but reet;
Th' reeson we've met heer th' neet ye ken is weel is me
It's for te help wor men te pae for the band it Tanfeeld Lee.

Chorus:
Thares big drums en cornits, tenor orns en bass;
Then thares two ufoamioms there's nowt cin them surpass.
Elang we two bumbardins, thare te tuaik thor torn;
Trambones en baritons en one flugil orn.

Th' vary beest thits in the feeld thor shoor te run awae,
Th' little dogs il grunge en bark wen the band begins te plae.
The men en wives il dance en sing th' bairns il run te see,
Thail plae th' troon te stop te heer th' band it Tanfeeld Lee.

Chorus

If ye gan te West Peltin te Pit Hill or th' Sykes
Cum back ower be Stanla th' Hobsin or the Dykes
Yil heer thim boast eboot thor bands but seun we'l let thim see,
Thit we cin rais e champyen band e wor awn it Tanfeeld Lee.

Chorus

Sum e theese big instruments is vary ard te blaw
But if yil oanly parseveer en keep eway yor jaw
En watch th points e musick we yor teechers aul agree,
Vary seun yil plae sum tuens we th' band it Tanfeeld Lee.

Chorus

There's credit due te Mistor Goice, he's lent e helping hand;
His sais his honist workin' men dis disarv e band
It band contests aul roond eboot aw hope we'l liv te see
Aul th' prises browt ewae we th' band it Tanfeeld Lee.

Chorus

Colliery Bands – such as the one formed in Tanfield Lea – were one of the great mining traditions in County Durham. Here are two local Silver Prize Bands:

South Moor Colliery, Silver Prize Band. Winners of the Grand Shield at Crystal Palace in 1907.

Craghead Colliery Silver Prize Band.

TANFIELD BRAIKE

This was written by Tommy Armstrong and to be sung to the tune of 'The Blaydon Races'. One part of the story is similar to that in 'Blaydon Races' in so much as the wheel came off the brake but otherwise it differs considerably. In 1869, before motorisation, a brake was a horse drawn coach used for transporting people. This song is still performed by folk singers.

A horse drawn brake laden with people.

'Twis in the munth iv Awgist, in hiteteen sixty-nine,
Aw thowt thit aw wid hev e ride, th' mornen wis se fine;
So aw catch't th' braik it Tanfield, before it went eway,
Te hev e ride inte th' toon, just te spend th' day.

Chorus:
Oh! dear, oh! ye shud'ard them shoot.
Aud Bessy Ferguson dabb'd ipon hor snoot;
Nan Smith wis lyen on the top e' Meggy Waik,
She sais she'll not forget th' day th' wheel cum off the braik.

We set away fra Tanfield before he gat his lode,
But thore wis plenty waitin' for him ipon the rode;
Wi' men fokes en wumen fokes, th' braik wis nearly fill'd,
We adin't getten far eway, te we wor nearly kill'd.

Chorus

Thare wis fowerteen that day drivon off thor crack –
Bill Car, Jack Car, Graim, en Coffee Jack;
Th' wumen fokes wis tauken eboot baicon bein' se cheep,
Wen aul it once th' wheel cum off, en cowpt is aul iv e heep.

Chorus

Wen Coffee Jack fell te th' ground he started for te sweer,
Is seun is he cud speek, he shooted, "What's th' mattor heer?"
Graim wis lyen speechless, en Coffee lost hees hat,
En if he adin't fund it he wis gan te rib aud Mat.

Chorus

'Twas ard to see th' wumen fokes e gannen te th' toon –
One shoots, "Aw've lost me hat," enuther rove hor goon;
"That's nowt for ye te tauk eboot aw's warse than that mesel."
Sais Janey Wood, "Aw've lost me porse, en smash't me umborel."

Chorus

Aw felt for Nanny Wilkinson, she gat e nasty crack,
Jack Car fell cross-leg'd reet on Nanny's back;
That wis accidental, but he dorty'd aul her goon,
If thae adn't got th' weel put on, she wad ridden im te th' toon.

Chorus

Th' drivor lost hees senses, en didden't naw ware te gan,
So he teuk 'ad e Coffee's heed, en shoots wo oi maw man;
Coffee struck oot we th' left, he appined te miss hees mark,
Eh muaid th' blud flee fres th' snoot e poor aud Bessy Clark.

Chorus

Coffee sais, "Let's drive eway; jump in en tuaik yor seet."
Graim sais, "We cannit gan until th' wheel's put reet."
Coffee sais, "It's nonsense; aw'll tell ye wat te dee:
Put th' lowse wheel in th' braik, en gan te th' toon we three.

Chorus

We sent eway for Stoker, he lived at Sunnyside,
We ad te get th' wheel put on before we gat e ride;
He wasn't lang e putint reet, en then we set eway,
We brockin ribs en flatten'd snoots, we spent e jolly day.

Spoken: Th' time th' blacksmith wis putten on th' wheel, aw pickt up fower young pillas. Aw thowt thae wor bags e sawdust. Coffee sais: "Tommy, them's Bussils." Aw thowt, for cureosity, aw wad open e one oot en see wat wis inside – proper paunshop. Aw gat a fower hippens, e bairn's slipper, e gimlick, e black leed brush, shoo horn, a pair e stockens, en Aud Moor's Alminack; so aw tied them up, en we aul began to sing th' korus.

Chorus

TRIMDON GRANGE EXPLOSION

On the afternoon of the 16th February 1882, a gas explosion took place at Trimdon Grange Colliery, about eight miles from Durham City, causing the death of 74 men and boys. Tommy Armstrong wrote this ballad soon afterwards and it is still sung by many folk singers and choirs.

Following the tragedy at the Twin Towers of the World Trade Centre in New York, USA on the 11th September 2001, the Trimdon Folk Group 'Skerne' recorded a CD of this song. The proceeds of the sales were donated to the funds which were set up in aid of the survivors and relatives of the victims of the tragedy[18]. Tommy would certainly have approved of this charitable act.

Let us not think of tomorrow lest we disappointed be;
All our joys may turn to sorrow as we all may daily see.
Today we may be strong and healthy but how soon there comes a
    change,
As we may learn from the explosion that has been at Trimdon Grange.

Men and boys left home that morning for to earn their daily bread,
Little thought before that evening that they'd be numbered with the
    dead.
Let us think of Mrs Burnett, once had sons but now has none,
By the Trimdon Grange explosion, Joseph, George and James are gone.

February left behind it what will never be forgot;
Weeping widows, helpless children may be found in many a cot,
Homes that once were blest with comfort, guided by a father's care,
Now are solemn, sad and gloomy since the father is not there.

Little children, kind and loving, from their homes each day would
    run
For to meet their father's coming, as each hard day's work was done.
Now they ask if father's left them, then the mother hangs her head;
With a weeping widow's feelings, tells the child that "father's dead."

God protect the lonely widow; help to raise each drooping head;
Be a father to the orphans; never let them cry for bread.
Death will pay us all a visit; they have only gone before;
We may meet the Trimdon victims where explosions are no more.

Trimdon Grange Colliery Lodge Banner.

TH' WHEELBARROW MAN

This is one of the works of Tommy Armstrong which tells about a man pushing a wheelbarrow from Dundee to London via Newcastle and the receptions he got at both of those places.

Right: The Albert Institute in Dundee.

YIL aul heh ard e Gimmy Gordin ganen freh Dundee,
He wis oot e wark en cudint keep his wife en familee,
Aul he got wen on th' road he reely did disarv;
He sade thit he wid raithor dee than let his bairney's starv.
It wis in November, en ipon th' second dae,
Wen Gordin en hees weelbarrow fixt te set ewae;
Butchers, grocors, draipors, stopt thor wark te gan en see
Gordin start for Lundin wiv hees barrow freh Dundee.

Spoken: Wen Gimmy wis riddy for th' road he sais, "Gid dae for a wee, stand back ye bairney's," th' road wis cleerd en Gimmy sade.

Chorus:
Heers of te Lundin en yid bettor clear th' wae
Aw want to be it yem aguain ipon th' Nue Yeer's dae.
If aw wis once ipon th' road awl muaik me barrow gan
Awl let thim see thit aws th' champyon weelbarrow man.

Gimmy en his barrow went it such e clivor stile
Th' bairens aul ran eftor im for lump ebuv e mile
Sum wis pullen at his cote, en runen biv hees side,
Shooting "Gimmy, stop th' cairt, en let us hev a ride."
Gimmy teuk nee heed e them he still kept weelen on;
En wiv a champyon stroke or two freh them he seun wis gone.
Thae shooted, "Gan on, Gimmy lad," is far is thae cud see,
Th' bairnes aul declaird thit Gordin muaid his barrow flee.

Spoken: Wen he gat oot e seet e th' spectators he ad five minits blaw, en hees nose cleend, en e spit oot then he sais –

Chorus

When Gimmy landed in Neucasil he wis welcum thare,
He sais he nivor seed se mony fokes it Glasgow fair.
He neethor seed e hoose or shop for thare wis such e thrang,
Th' bobbies ad te muaik a rode for im te pass elang.
Rotten eggs en orangis, clarts en lumps e breed,
Brocken pipes, en baccy chows wis stottin off his heed.
Sum wid crie oot wat e shem en strugil ard te see,
Gordon th' weelbarrow-man, cumen freh Dundee.

Spoken: Gimmy stopt aul neet e Nuecasil, the next mornen thare wis hundrids waiten te see im off, he thenkt thim for thair kindness, then he lifted his barrow frev its int legs en sais –

Chorus

Wen Gimmy gat te Lunden he wis met we greet sorprise.
Th' cocknies stud en luckt it im is if he wasint wise.
Thae put nee muny in his box thave arts is ard is stuain,
He sais he'l dee in Scotlind twice before he'l gan eguain.
He sais he ad sum hevy daes we wet en wind en snaw.
But what he teuk ipon th' rode we'l nivor get te naw,
But hees landed yem en glad he is his wife en bairns te see,
En he thenks th' fokes ipon th' Tine for being see kind en free.

Spoken: Gimmy sais, if it wis barrow shuving esteed e boat pulling he wid be champyon. He wants te shuv Hanlon or Beech on th' suaim wattor. If he defeeted Saw Dust Gack, en Bob Black, an ansor throo th' Sunda Companion will be etendid tee –

Tower Bridge, London.

Bridges over the River Tyne at Newcastle.

PART FOUR

Six Unpublished Works of Thomas Armstrong

Six previously unpublished works of Thomas Armstrong which are referred to at Beamish Regional Resource Centre.

Two of the works are now published with the kind permission of the Beamish Regional Resource Centre where they are held. They have not been previously published or found elsewhere.

> a) Sewing Meeting.
> b) The Unhappy Couple.

Two other works held at the Beamish Regional Resource Centre have also been found in old newspapers and the Centre is pleased for them to be published now. They have not been previously published or found elsewhere.

> c) Jack Reckonen.
> d) Old Dolly Cook and her Family.

Two other works of Thomas Armstrong which have been found in newspapers are referred to at Beamish Regional Resource Centre but no copies are held there. The Resource Centre is pleased for them to be published now and they have not been published or found elsewhere.

> e) Geordie Broon.
> f) Neglectful Sally.

A SEWING MEETING

This poem, in handwritten form, is held at Beamish Regional Resource Centre, which has kindly given permission for it to be transcribed for this book. Written and signed Tommy Armstrong, it is of quite a serious nature which is a variation on most of his works that tend to be light hearted and humorous.

No trace can be found of this poem having been published elsewhere.

Mr Swainston my dear Sir
You may have done such like before
For fear you never do it more
Be kind enough to read this oer
      Unto your congregation

It was with pleasure and delight
That I sat down these lines to write
Not Members only to invite
But every person here tonight
      Accept this invitation

Tomorrow there is going to be
A sewing meeting and a tea
The givers will be glad to see
Every one in Tanfield Lea
      Mary Jane and Kitty

At No 11 Edwart (sic) Street
All are welcome for to meet,
Those that come will find a seat
Those that dont will miss a treat
      And that will be a pitty (sic)

Our Christian Sisters does their best
With all the power they are posessed
They toil until they cannot rest
With sewing they are so distressed
      So anxious and so fervent (sic)

God bless the work they have begun
And when the victorys fairly won
And the last thread of life is spun
The Lord will say to each well done
      Thou good and faithful servant

We all should help with heart & hand
The travellers to immanuels (sic) land
Therefore I hope you understand
This is to help the Mission Band
  Every one remember

The females say theyll raise a drum
To do so it will take a sum
The young the old the deaf the dumb
Every one be sure to come
  On the 8th day of September

It is a rule in such a case
When each partaker takes his place
Around the table face to face
Some Christian Brother says the grace
  That is all the telling

When tea is done and tabels (sic) clear
The Mission Band we then shall hear
Play some tunes each heart to cheer
When time for bed we'll disapear (sic)
  Each one to their own dwelling

Yours Truly
Tommy Armstrong
Tanfield Lea
Local Poat (sic)

A group of sewing ladies.

THE UNHAPPY COUPLE

This poem, in handwritten form, is held at Beamish Regional Resource Centre which has kindly given permission for a transcription to be used in this book. It is headed 'The Unhappy Couple' but is not actually signed by Tommy Armstrong. However, it is assumed to be the song referred to in a letter from an acquaintance of Tommy's to the local newspaper in 1916[1].

The relevant part of the letter reads, "To Hear Mr McCrum and Tommy Armstrong sing 'The Unhappy Couple' was delightful. If you were in the dumps when they commenced, your bad temper was soon gone. No one could resist laughing."

No trace can be found of this item having been published elsewhere.

My name is Jemmy Robinson my age is sixty three,
And ah once was as happy as a man cud ever be.
But the priest of Bishop Auckland hes surely taun me doon,
Since he's putting me a cavil in alang wi Mary Broon.

She drinks and she thinks that ah shudn't have a quart,
And winnet wash her hands when she' mixing up a tart.
We've been married thirty year and she never combed her heed,
And its only cost her twopence since ah married her for thread.

She had the world for'd a loaf she couldn't baike,
And breakfast, supper, dinner ah got nowt but water caike.
Her stockings is awl holey and she says she cannot darn,
She cannot set a button on and says she winnet learn.

She gans oot in the morning and gossips all the day,
Ah knaw it isn't reet to carry on in such a way.
But if she disn't try for to mend her wicked ways,
I'll be a single fellow the remainder of my days.

JACK RECKONEN/JACK'S RECKONING

This is a story by Tommy Armstrong ridiculing the various deductions from the coal hewers pay. Whilst it is written as a 'nonsense' story, the theme behind it is probably near the truth of what took place. The version in dialect was in the local newspaper in 1913 showing Tommy's address as Tanfield Lea[2].

A second version in standard English is in the form of a broadsheet at Beamish Museum. The first paragraph varies from the dialect version and at the end, shows Tommy's address as 1 Oak Terrace, Tantobie. It is likely that Tommy produced the dialect version first then transferred it into standard English for the broadsheet some time afterwards. This is supported by the Tantobie address being shown on the broadsheet, which is where Tommy moved to from Tanfield Lea later in his life, as explained in Chapter 6: 'The Character and Alleged Drunkard'.

First Version

JACK RECKONEN OR TH' NUE PITMAN

It was two thousand, five hundred en thorty-sivon 'eer befor th' borth iv Adim it e plaice th' caul Nonentity. In th' parish is Understanden, e chep th' caul Jack Bovril thout e wid hev e start e th' pits. It wis th' time wen th' big muny wis on. He started at the Ging or Snap Collory on th' thorty-sivonth dae e Novaipril. Wen his marrow com' in bye e th' back shift, e sais te Jack, "Be shoor en gan te th' reckonen th' neet , en the owormin il tell th' hoo monny yards en scors we hev; en think 'im on eboot yon hitch en helpin up." Jack sais, "Aul reet, gud mornen."

Wen Jack gat yem, he sais te thair Meg, "Caul me up it three o'clock, aws ganen te th' reckonen th' neet." "Th' reckonen," sais Meg, "wat's that? Aw warned it's th' Store Hall. We ist for? Wat time dist gan in? Awl gan we th'." "Get awae," sais Jack, "Thoo disnt understand. It's wat th' caul th' pitman's reckonen; awl get te naw th' neet wet awl hev for me pae th' morn neet." "Oh, aw see," sais Meg, "hoo much dis th' think thoo'l heh te tuaik this time?" Jack sais, "Aw canit sae exactly, but aw shud hev three pund, six or sivon. Aw wid like te hev e pair e pit shoos this time, but awl gan en see."

Wen Jack gat te th' office he sais, "Noo maister, wat fettil th' neet; awve nivor seen ye this week; aw thowt yid meby geten th' infloonensy. Auve 'ad th' teethwark aul dae; aw wish aw 'ad thim pade for, thor false teeth. Bob Robysin's wife fell inte th' guttor th' dae en broke her leg, but she's not much warse. Just befor aw cam' awae freh yem, two cheps wiv e cab com' te tuaik Bessy Broon te th' Sylim, but thae gat th' rang hoose, en thae teuk Jainy Cooper en thare's nowt th' mattor wiv her, poor sowl. Is this reckonen neet maistor?" "Aw think thoo hes reckonen," sais th' maistor.

Lisson te me e bit. Thoo hes six score six e coals, en nine tubs owerwite muaiks six score fifteen; thares one tub set oot, fower tubs

A hewer in a County Durham pit.

lade oot, that leevs six score ten, it siven shillen e score, muaiks th'
munny for coals two pund five en sivonpince; sixpence e score for
helping up, two shillen e score for worken wet, fower yards e narrow
bord it tenpence e yard, two yards e winen heedwise it one en fipins e
yard, five yards e wall it one en tupins e yard, ten yards e side coal it
sixpence e yard, hauf e croon for yon dip hitch - aw forgat th' rent, but
awl put it next time; that muaiks th' munny three pund ten en
thripins." "Thenk ye, maistor, auve a bettor pae than aw thowt aw wid
hev. Dinet forget th' rent next time. Wor Meg will be pleased. Gud neet,
maistor."

   "Stop," sais th' maistor, "te thoo get th'off-tuaiks." "Offtuaiks" sais
Jack. "Nivor mind them. Aws quite content. Aw kin get them next
time." "Lisson," sais th' maistor, "thar's siven shillen for poothor en
candils, tupins for th' pick sharpor, sixpence for hose en coals,
ninepence for th' doctor, sixpence for wattor, hitepence for th' weiman,
en hauf e croon thee gat ower much last time; en two shillen for th'
hospital, fower shillen for striken it th' putter, two shillen for e shaft en
pick, that leevs two pund ten en tupins for thee te draw th' morn neet."
Jack sais, "If aud nawn this aw wadint e cumd. If thee ad enothor try it
wid be awl off-tuaiks."

Wen Jack gat yem, he sais te Meg, "Awl nivor gan te th' reckonen again." "Hoos that?" sais Meg. "Aw had three pund ten en thripince it forst, en wen aw cum ewae aw had oanly two pund ten en tupins. He kept one pund en a penny off for what he cauld off-tuaiks." Meg sais, "Th' dorty scoundrel, awl gan te th' reckonen mesel next time, en if he starts wiv hees off-tuaiks, awl tuaik hees nose off his faice. Let's see if we kin pae wor wae. Thare's one pund six en e penny for grosorys; butcher, fifteen en tupins; sewing machine man two en sixpence; one shillen for milk; nine pince for th' Union; one en sixpence for inshoorince; two shillen for the tailor; fourpince for yest; that leevs tenpince te get e pair e pit shoos with. Wat e shem; Nee beer."

THOMAS ARMSTRONG
Pitman's Poet, Tanfield Lea

Second Version

JACK'S RECKONING

MR EDITOR

A few years ago a man I knew well, a Joiner to trade, commenced to hew coals at East Tanfield Colliery. He was in the fore shift after he had been on a while. When his marrow came in on the back shift, he said to Jack, "Be sure and go to the reckoning tonight. The overman will tell you how many yards and scores you have, and think him on about the Dip hitch, and helping up." At that time, it was fortnightly pays. Miners had to go to the overman's house or office and he would tell you what the pay was for you to draw on the following night. Jack says, "All right. Good Morning."

When Jack got home, he says to his wife, Meg, "Call me up at three o'clock, I am going to the reckoning tonight." "The reckoning" says Meg, "What's that, it will likely be at the Store Hall. Who is it for, what time does it go in, I will go with you." Meg thought the reckoning was a concert. "Get away" says Jack, "You don't understand it. I will get to know tonight what I will have for my pay tomorrow night." "Oh I see" says Meg, "How much do you think you will have to take for pay?" Jack says, "I cannot say exactly, but I should have three pound six or seven. I would like to have a pair of pit shoes this time but I will go and see."

When Jack got to the office, he was beat how to introduce himself to the overman. He had never been at the reckoning before, in he goes and says, "Well master, what fettle tonight. I have never seen you this week, I thought perhaps you had got the influenza. Just before I came from home, I saw two men with a cab to take Bessie Brown to the Asylum, but they got to the wrong house and took Mary Cooper, and nothing ailed her poor soul. Bob Watson's wife fell into the gutter today and broke her leg, but she's not much worse. Is this reckoning night Master?"

The Master says, "Listen to me awhile, you have six score six of coal, and nine tubs of overweight that makes six score fifteen. One tub set out, four tubs laid out that leaves six score ten, at seven shillings a score, makes thy money for coals, two pound five and seven pence. Sixpence a score for helping up, two shillings a score for working wet. Four yards of narrow board at tenpence a yard, two yards of winning headways at one and five pence a yard. Five yards of wall at one and twopence a yard. Ten yards of side coal at sixpence a yard. Half a crown for dip hitch, I forgot the rent but I will put it in next time. That makes thy money three pounds ten and threepence." "Thank you master, I have a better pay that I thought, my wife Meg will be pleased, don't forget the rent next time. Good night Master."

"Stop" says the master "until you get the offtakes." "Offtakes" says Jack. "Never mind them, I can get them next time, I am quite content." "Listen to me" says the master, "there's seven shillings for powder and candles; twopence for the pick sharper and sixpence for house and coal. Ninepence for the doctor. Sixpence for water. Ninepence for the weighman. Half a crown you got over much last time. Two shillings for the hospital. Two shillings for picks and shafts and four shillings for striking at a putter. That leaves two pounds ten and twopence for you to draw for your pay tomorrow night." Jack says, "If I had known you were going to treat me like this, I would not have come. If you had another try it will be all offtakes."

When he got home, he said to his wife, "Meg, I will never go to the reckoning again." "What for?" says Meg. I had three pound ten and threepence at first and when I came away, I had two pound ten and twopence, he kept one pound and a penny off for what he called offtakes." Meg says, "The dirty scoundrel, I'll go to the reckoning myself next time and if he starts with his offtakes, I'll take his nose off his face. Lets us see if we can pay our way, there's one pound six and a penny for groceries, fifteen and twopence for the butcher, two and sixpence for the sewing machine man, one shilling for milk, ninepence for the Union, one and sixpence for insurance, two shillings for the tailer and fourpence for yeast. That leaves tenpence to get a pair of pit shoes. What a shame, it's a blessing you are teetotal."

TOMMY ARMSTRONG
Pitman Poet, 1 Oak Terrace, Tantobie

OLD DOLLY COOK
AND HER FAMILY

This was a 'nonsense story' written by Tommy Armstrong, most likely about a fictional family and it appeared in the local newspaper in 1913[3].

A handwritten version headed "The History of Dolly Cook & her family" is held at Beamish Museum. It varies slightly from the version in the newspaper, is not in Tommy's handwriting and is not 'signed off' at the end. There is every likelihood that it was transcribed from the newspaper version by someone who made slight errors but deliberately altered the final sentence to read "Apply to Mr Buckthurn apple street or Tommy Armstrong Pilgrim Street."

Old Dolly Cook was the mother of two sons and one daughter. Her husband was a single man, with a dark beard and grey whiskers. His left eye was on the right side of his left leg. He wore a muffler made up of six months dividends, tied round his left arm to keep his neck warm. He was lost at sea while riding in a railway carriage on his way to Morpeth to see his grandmother, who was scalded to death in America by falling upstairs while coming down.

This was the beginning of Dolly's happiness. Her eldest son left home at the beginning of next week. He was stark naked with his father's clothes on. He had his face shaved hairy and his hair cut curly. He had a large lump at the back side of his forehead and a dark moustache on his chin end. He wore a pair of wellington shoes, laced at the top of his head to keep his hair on. He can only speak with one eye; the other has lost its speech. He was last seen going through Dipton with the School Board Man on his back, enquiring for Consett Police Station to give himself in charge of Dr. Bruce of Shotley Bridge, to be vaccinated at the back of his neck for eating plum pudding without a licence. He has not been heard of since next Saturday.

Dolly heard that her son had been apprehended at West Stanley by P.C. Staff and Buttons for stealing three coke ovens, the property of the Hen and Chicken Company. He had one under each arm and one in his waistcoat pocket, inquiring for a pawnshop in West Stanley. He was taken into Rowe's cook-shop and compelled to eat eleven tea-cakes without taking a bite. He was then close confined in the open air, where he died three days before the breath went out. He was buried next Friday; lift at four, bury at three.

Friends please neglect this invitation. Her youngest son was the eldest. He was born three days before his elder brother. His mother was absent when he was born. He left home next Monday in search of nothing to do. He went up with the down train. He sees best with his right ear, the other one being bloodshot. He wore a round square hat composed of Store checks. He listens with his mouth. He has only two fingers and one thumb on his left foot. He wore a swallow-lapped jacket. He gets up before he goes to bed. He gets his breakfast first thing at night and his supper last thing in the morning.

The postman came this morning with a letter yesterday, saying that he was shovelling wind off the railway at Lintz Green Station, and was paid every week, once a month, quarterly at the year's end. Any person giving correct inflammation as to leave him alone, shall receive three months imprisonment for not minding their own business.

Dolly and her daughter are going to shift higher down last Thursday to a larger house with two rooms less than the one they are living in. It will be in the middle of the street, at the top end, close to the bottom. They are going to commence with the following words above the door: "Useful men wanted; must be young and sound to work for two ladies. Apply personally or come yourself. You will find the bell at the back side of the front door. Any further inflammation wanted, apply to Mrs Cook, Slipper and Boot Street, or Thomas Armstrong, Pilgrim Street.

Inside a Durham miner's cottage.

GEORDIE BROON

This funny and very long poem is about a man who repeatedly got drunk and beat his wife but he lived to rue the day.

It was written by Tommy Armstrong and appeared in the local newspaper in 1913[4] but apart from that, there is no trace of it having been published elsewhere. A poem called 'Drunken Geordie' is listed at Beamish Regional Resource Centre as one of Tommy's unpublished works and probably refers to this poem but there is not a copy at the Resource Centre.

Thare wis a varry drunken chep, his nuaim was Geordie Broon,
Aw winnit try to raise him up, nor try te run him doon;
He was a collory blacksmith, aw often 'ard it sade,
Thor nivvor was a bettor man than Geordie tiv his trade.
Neebody shud be bettor off than Geordie en his wife,
But throo intoxicaition drink he led e retshid life.
Meggy yuse te sit en fret when he was on the spree,
Becaws she new wen he com yem wat he wis sure te dee.

Meggy ad a Bible, in which she teuk a pride,
Which she oftin sat en read wen Geordie wis outside.
Wi sweld fuaic en blackend eyes, she oftin sat te reed,
Ware Geordie oftin kickt hor aboot th' fuaice en heed.
Wen ivvor Geordie gat much drink, it yuse te drive him mad,
En then wen he cum yem et neets, he yuse te show his bad.
He yuse to fell hor te th' flor en yuse buaith hands en feet,
Befor' aws deun aal tell ye hoo he met wiv his defeet.

Meg ad a canny neibor, hor nuaim wis Ganny Lee,
One dae she sais te Meggy, just be advised bi me.
If thoo'll dee is aw want thi, awi seun devise e plan,
Then eftor that yor Geordie will becum a sober man.
Meggy sais, "Te cure him aw reely wad be glad,
But aw wadint like te hort him, altho' he is see bad.
Aw wud scratch oot awl hees deun since aw becom his wife
If he wad be teetoatil the remainder of his life."

"He's off aguain this mornen," sais Meg te Ganny Lee,
He cudint tuaik his breckfist wen he luckt it me.
Wen he saw me ees wis black, he sais, "Hev aw deun that?"
She ansord "Yis." "Wei then" he sais, "Reech me coat an' hat."
On ganen oot wen he gat drest, he stopt and sade te me,
"Meg will thoo giv me sixpence, this is the final spree.
Te landlords en landladies awl for ivvor bid edew,
En awl intoxicaition drink, thit muaiks me strike it thoo."

141

Enjoying a drink!

"Di th' giv' him sixpence to set him on th' spree?"
"Aw dorsint dee nee uthor," sais Meg te Ganny Lee.
"Varry well," sais Ganny, "Thoo'l git it back th' neet,
He'll likely black thi uthor ee en that'll sarve thi reet.
Te cure him of his druckiness aw reely wad be glad,
Becaws aw naw wen he cums yem he will be full e bad.
But if he strikes it thoo th' neet, wen sober he will see,
Hoo a man cin be deceevd wen he's been en th' spree."

"Varry weel," sais Meggy, "Just dee wat thoo thinks best;"
Then Ganny gat th' pos stick en 'ad it nicely drest.
She sais, "Get me e tornip, eethor white or sweed,
En then get me e neetcap, te muaik e fancy heed."
She put th' pos stick inte bed, en lapt it up wi clais,
"My word, but thoos e buety, thoos e pictor," Ganny sais.
"Aw winnit tie thi hat strings, thoo hesn't lang te lie,
He's sure te pull thi heed off, it leest he's sure te try."

"Let him cum," sais Ganny "En start his gam th' neet,
We'll see him in his aginy th' mornen it dae leet.
He'll not be lang e cumin noo, so lets buaith thee en me,
Leeve th' door ipon th' sneck, en nivvor mind th' kee."
Ewae th' went te Ganny's en just gat sitten doon,
Wen thae ard him shooten, "Thae caal me Geordie Broon,
Wat aw wid dee wen aw gat yem aw've oftin sade befor',
But wen aw de get yem the neet, wor Meggy is nee mor."

Geordie com is yuseiwil, sweering' te th' door,
He tumeld in en flung his coat en hat ipon th' flor.
He sais, "This is th' final spree, this is th' final neet,
Get on thi nees, en sae thi prairs thoo'l nivvor see daeleet.
Be sharp, dee wat aw tell thar, or else off goes th' heed.
Inuther time awl ax thi thet thoos numbord wi' th' deed."
Becaws he gat nee ansor, he wis wild ipon th' flor,
Frothen it th' mooth he then began te luk for hor.

It last he lukt tewards th' bed, "Oh, thoos thare," sais he.
"Thoos been lyen awl this time, en nivvor anserd me.
Get up en get thi clais on, aw winit ax thi thrice.
Get up," he sais. Nee anser still; he sais, "Aw've axt thi twice,
This is th' thord time en th' last, get up, thoos surely deed."
In vengince Geordie went, en grabbed hor bi th' heed.
He browt ewae th' neetcap, expectin' it wis hor,
Doon he went wi such a thud, his lenth ipon th' flor.

Mad wi pashon wen he fell, he swor en rowld iboot,
He sais, "If aw wis up eguain, thoo'l wish thoo 'ad been oot."
He strugild hard, en grumild sair aboot his nasty fall,
He sais, "Aw heh th' neetcap, aw'l heh th' heed en awl."
Geordie gat onte th' flor, en yused buaith hans en feet,
En kept tauken te th' pos stick is if he wasn't reet.
He kickt th' pos stick off th' bed; he sais, "Noo, off thoo goes."
He struck en kickt his fancy wife until he broak his toes.

It daeleet in th' mornen, Meg sais te Ganny Lee,
"Aw wundor hoo he's ganen on, let's buaith gan in en see."
Wen thae went in, there Geordie sat, awl corld up in e chare.
Ganny sais, "Wat fettil, noo aw warnd thoos stiff en sair?"
"Me hans is sweld like dumplins en me feet's the suaim," he sais,
Ganny sais, "It sarves thi reet, thoo'l mebby mend thi wais,
Twis me thit muaid thi suffor, te muaik thi change thi life.
So aw teuk yor Meggy's pos stick en aw muaid e fancy wife".

Ganny gat th' pos stick en lade it on th' flor.
She put th' cap en turnip on is thae had been befor,
"There she is," sais Ganny, "wivoot a broaken bone,
Last neet thoo kickt hor oot of bed which muaid thi sigh en mone."
"That'll dee," sais Geordie, "Is long is aw remane,
E pos stick nor e turnip shall nivvor caws me pane."
Geordie's wife en Ganny Lee buaith offord up a prair,
En Geordie sined th' temporince pledge, wen sitten in a chare.

A Poss Stick comprising of a heavy piece of wood with a stalk and heavy foot which used to thump dirty clothes in a tub of soap and water so as to wash them.

NEGLECTFUL SALLY

This is a comical poem by Tommy Armstrong about a man and his wife who both liked their alcohol but she more than him. It was written by Tommy Armstrong and was found in the local newspaper in 1913[5].

In a little colliery village there lived a man and wife,
If ye lissen ye shill heer hoo thae went on in life.
Thae had nee little bairns, thae wis only him en hor,
Th' skuel bord man wis nivvor seen et Sally Jopson's dor.
Sally wis a jolly sowl, and Jacky wis th' suaim,
Thae were eether buaith awae, or else buaith it yem.
Sally liked hor whiskey, en Jacky liked his beer,
Wat muaid them join th' temporince aul trie to let ye heer.

One Sunda' neet thae buaith sat doon, is thae did ivory neet,
Jacky's fancy suppor was beer en breed en meet.
Sally didn't fancy that, therefor she wadint hed,
She liked a glass or two e rum before she went to bed.
Thae sat en drank till late it neet, then Sally got th' torn,
She sais, "Aul tell th' wat aul dee, aul wesh en buaik th' morn;
Aul git up wen thoo gits up, the caulor cauls at three,
En if aw divvent heer him caul, be sure en caul e me."

Th' cauler cauled en Sall en Jack wis suin upon th' flor,
She dressed that quick, Jack for a while just stood en lukt at hor.
He sais, "Thoos meant for business we getting up se seun,"
"Yis," sais Sall, "when thoo cums yem, aul cleaned en duen."
Jacky gat his breckfist, en then went off to work,
Sally put hor heed ootside, "My word," she sais, "it's dark.
It isn't fower o'clock yit en aw haven't any clais,
Aul hev enuther glass o rum, en then aul start," she sais.

She placed hor little bottle en hor chair beside th' fire,
She sais, "Oh you've aul th' comfort thit a woman can desire."
She teuk hor bottle off th' shelf, en got a china cup,
She didn't like a wine glass cause it only held a sup.
Th' fire wis warm, th' rum wis hot, yet Sally gamely sat,
Drinken rum en tauken tiv hor little fancy cat.
Th' clock, "Aul right," she sais, "Aul hev e start just noo,
Thors plenty time te wesh en bake en hev a glass or two."

She drank hor rum until it teuk possession ov hor heed,
She sais, "Aul hev a start just noo wor nearly cot a breed."
She teuk th' bottle en th' cup en put them buaith away,
She sais, "Auve left a little sup te sarve another day."
She tried te get up off the chair but she fell wi' being see numb,
She coupt th' table en th' chair en spilt her lovely rum.
She broke the bottle en the cup, en something warse thin that,
When she fell she dabbed upon en killed hor fancy cat.

There she lay upon th' flor, just like somebody deed,
En wen she hard th' clock strike, she lifted up hor heed.
"Good gracious me, is that th' time," then doon aguen she lay,
"Aul let th' breed en weshen gan until another day."
She rowled horsel aboot the mat en suen began te snore,
En nivvor wakened up until their Jack coom te th' dor.
Eftor worken hard aul day, te keep hissel en hor,
It wis a caud reception for te find hor on th' flor.

Wen he com yem, he stud emais'd, en luckt aul roond aboot,
He saw thor was nee dinnor muaid, en thit th' fire wis oot.
He saw th' tuaibil en th' chair buaith lyen on th' flor,
Wen Jack wis tryen te put thim reet, Sall gave an awful snor.
"Aye, snore way, thoo drucken slut, that's wat thoo cairs for me,
Aw cum freh work th' day, te neethor dinnor nor tea.
Thoo wis gan te wesh en buaik en be aul nicely deun,
Aw thowt thoo'd deun rang th' day wi getten up se seun."

Jack sais, "Aul muaik th' fire on, en muaik mesel sum tee,"
Sally spoak up is she lae, "Aye, muaik e sup for me.
Th' hoose is gannen roond wi me, ma heed is like ti split,
En if thoo wants me reet eguain, aul tell thi wat te get.
Dip e cloot emang caud watter, en put it on mau broo,
Or else aul dee, en that will be e serious job for thoo."
Jack gat e pail e wattor, en throo it on hor heed,
He sais, "Thooll seun be bettor, or else thooll seun be deed."

Sally jumpt ipon th' flor, en began te screem en shoot,
Jack sais, "Thoo tell'd ma for te git some wattor en a cloot.
Auve getten thoo th' wattor, thoo kin git th' cloot thisel."
Sall sais, "Oh dear, aam fainten," en doon eguain she fell.
Jack sais, "Thoo'd bettor gan te bed," he tried te raise hor up,
Twis there he saw th' broken bottle en th' china cup.
He gat hor lifted inte bed, en lookt tewards th' mat,
En there, behold, he saw thit she had killed thor fancy cat.

Sall got up next mornen, but wis feeble aul th' day,
Jack sais te Sall, "Tuaik notice wat aam ganen te say.
Th' fire wis oot, en nee dinnor muaid, en thoo lay on th' mat,
Thoo broak e bottle en a cup, en killed wor fancy cat.
Thoo broak e bottle en a cup, such wark is this il nivvor dee,
Therefor if thoo intends te drink thee shanit stop wi me."
Sally sais, "Aul tuaik enoath aul nivvor drink eguain,"
Jack en Sall buaith sign'd th' pledge te leeve th' drink eluain.

PART FIVE

Ten Further Unpublished Works of Thomas Armstrong

Ten works of Thomas Armstrong found in local newspapers and which have not previously been published, nor has any reference been made to them elsewhere.

GATESHEAD POOR CHILDREN'S TRIP TO STANLEY, 5th JULY 1913

This poem was written by Tommy Armstrong to record the annual visit to Stanley of the poor children from Gateshead and to acknowledge the kindness towards them, by the people of Stanley.

It appeared in the local newspaper in 1913[1] but apart from that, there is no trace of it having been published elsewhere, either prior to or since that date.

While looking through 'West Stanley News' not many weeks ago,
I saw the Gateshead children's trip was coming to Shield Row.
And then from there to Stanley, where they have been before,
And of times have enjoyed themselves in a field behind the Store.

Six hundred little boys and girls came with the morning train,
To see the clothing which they wore filled every heart with pain.
Some had no stockings for to wear, no shoes upon their feet,
And looked as if some weeks had passed since they had ought to eat.

Our great Salvation Army Band agreed that morn to meet,
Those little ones down at Shield Row, and play them through the street.
And when the children all got placed, the Band began to play,
Three cheers went up from those around to see them march away.

Unto the Stanley tradesmen all, we must give every praise,
For helping those poor children in so many different ways.
Good boots and shoes, and stockings too, and other clothes as well,
Hats and caps, scarves and gloves, and more than I can tell.

The streets were packed on either side, each one had picked their stand,
To see those little children pass, and hear the Army band.
Two females stood close side by side, but neither seemed to speak,
And when they saw the children's clothes, the tears ran down each cheek.

The children say they love to come the Stanley folks to see,
They always are provided with all kinds of food and tea.
Each poor child gets a paper bag, with food to serve all day,
And each one has a portion left for them to take away.

Four thousand and eight hundred buns were baked by Mr Rowe,
The Stanley great confectioner, whom many people know.
He made six hundred pies with meat, to feed those hungry souls,
In all there were six thousand baked, buns, pies and sausage rolls.

The Poor Bairns Trip from Consett.

KELLOE DISASTER

On Thursday 6th May 1897, an underground flood occurred at East Hetton Colliery, Kelloe during which ten of the thirteen miners who were working down below, lost their lives. A Deputy Overman, Mr Morley, who was in another part of the seam, played a major part in the rescue of two miners – John Forster and John Stanton[2]. It was believed that the other eleven men were all dead but four days later, John Wilson was miraculously found alive – he had been hemmed in on higher ground[2].

Tommy Armstrong wrote this poem to commemorate the tragedy and in recognition of the bravery of the Deputy Overman, Mr Morley. Apart from the poem being in the local newspaper in 1897[3], there is no trace of it having been published elsewhere, either before or since that date.

Death has paid another visit to some miners while below.
At a place they call East Hetton, little o'er five weeks ago;
Thirteen miners, strong and hearty, left their homes the sixth of May,
Little thinking death was waiting soon to take their souls away.

It was on the Thursday evening, when those miners did descend,
For the bread of life to labour, far from home and earthly friends;
They like all good-hearted miners, each commenced to labour free –
All was right till Friday morning – until shortly after three.

Then, alas! a rush of water burst into the mine below,
And took those men away before it, any way it chose to go.
A deputy, the name of Morley, had descended underground
To examine working places; there he heard a rumbling sound.

He shouted to the men to "hurry, look for nothing, don't delay";
As he spoke, the water caught him, he was nearly washed away.
There he saw two workmen struggling – to save them there was
    little hope –
The only way that he could help them was to cast to them a rope.

He knew his life was in great danger, yet he could not pass these two;
He cast a rope and they both caught it, then John Morley pulled them
    through.
Quite exhausted, wet and suffering, they were drawn from underground;
How they did escape from drowning, people wonder all around.

To this noble-hearted hero there is every credit due;
On the brink of death he ventured such a noble act to do.
The masters of East Hetton Colliery, and the working men around,
All should honour noble Morley, for his bravery underground.

There were still eleven miners, hid from friends, entombed below,
None expected to be living, but it did not happen so;
While a batch of men undaunted were exploring down below,
They heard a voice come from the water, which encouraged them to go.

Onward they kept persevering, going along the engine plane,
Travelling to the waist in water, when they heard a voice again;
A few more steps and then John Wilson by those gallant men was
    found;
Only they can tell their meeting, in the water underground.

The exploring party took him in their arms uplifted high,
Bore him gently from the water to a place where it was dry;
From below they soon ascended; attended to by skilful men,
Now John Wilson is recovering, which leaves the number
    drowned as ten.

Ten brave-hearted men of labour became victims underground;
A week elapsed before nine bodies by those gallant men were found.
James Oliver was still a-missing, lifeless in the mine below,
Men of bravery found the body, on the 26th of May.

May the Widows and the children who have lost their earthly friend,
Trust in God and He will guide them through all trials to the end.
And when earthly toils are ended, may they meet on Canaan's shore
With those victims of East Hetton; there disasters are no more.

EAST HETTON COLLIERY DISASTER
6th MAY 1897

When the following men were killed by underground flooding

Garside, John, aged 51, Stoneman
Gibbon, Anthony, aged 41, Shifter
Hall, William, aged 50, Shifter
Hutchinson, Thomas, aged 49, Stoneman
Oliver, James, aged 42, Wasteman
Pearson, Edward, aged 50, Wasteman
Raine, John, aged 63, Wasteman
Robinson, Matthew, aged 26, Shifter
Roney, Thomas, aged 58, Shifter
Smith, Edward, aged 26, Shifter

Names of those who were killed in this disaster.

THE OLD MEN'S TRIP

FROM THE VICTORIA CLUB, WEST STANLEY

This poem, which is in two parts, was written by Tommy Armstrong. The first part which was found in the local newspaper in 1913[4], gave news of an impending trip for old men and explained how good a similar trip had been the previous year.

Tommy promised to report on the outcome of the trip and true to his word, the second part of the poem appeared in the newspaper three weeks later[5]. He wrote both parts of the poem in standard English but at the end of the second part, he wrote an account of some of the activities in dialect.

Apart from the two parts of this poem in the newspaper, no trace can be found of them having been published elsewhere, either before or since those dates.

(FIRST PART OF THE POEM)

The thirtieth day of August is drawing very near,
When the old men get their trip as they did last year.
The members of the Victoria Club all seem to take a pride,
In cheering up old people's hearts by giving them a ride.

We had a splendid trip last year, and I am proud to say,
That I was one amongst them that spent a happy day.
We set off from the Victoria Club upon a Saturday morn,
I thought it was the happiest day I've spent since I was born.

I've oft been asked the reason why I did not make a poem,
About the trip we had last year, when we arrived back home.
For my previous negligence I hope you'll me excuse,
When we return this year you'll see it in the 'Stanley News'.

I've got an invitation free to go with them again,
All being well I will be there, I hope it does not rain.
The Secretary (Thomas Curry) and President (William Clark),
Are going to see that each old man is 'tret' up to the mark.

Likewise the brave Committee men and other members too,
Are going to see if there is anything at all which they can do.
To help the old and feeble ones, and cheer them on their way,
We're depending on the Weather Clerk to send a splendid day.

The Sands and Pier, South Shields.

Marsden Grotto, South Shields.

THE OLD MEN'S TRIP TO SHIELDS

I promised in 'The Stanley News' that I would write a poem,
About the Old Men's Trip to Shields, if we got safely home.
We landed safe, therefore I'll try my promise to fulfil,
And tell you how we spent the day without any ill.

We set off from the Victoria Club between eight and nine,
The thirtieth morn of August, the sun did brightly shine.
Each man had made up his mind before we went away,
All to join in heart and soul and spend a happy day.

We had our photos taken before we went away,
How many there were in number I'm not prepared to say.
I know the group that was in front, each man sat on a seat,
The group that was behind them was standing on their feet.

I should have stood up in the front through being born so short,
I know I'm not good-looking, I just stood up for sport.
A tall man stood in front of me, and I could not change my place,
So should you find me in the group, you'll just see half a face.

On behalf of each old man, for the ride and for the grub,
I am requested for to thank the members of the Club.
And should they live till they are old, when us old men are gone,
May they be as kindly treat by the young men following on.

Mistor Editor, – Aal trie te tell ye sum e wor travils wen we gat te
Sheels. We gat thare aal reet, but nee wunder. Mistor Holmes, Tantoby
had th' job in hand te find th' braiks and drivers. What wi th' cairful
drivers en th' fine dae, it was grand.

Aal trie en tell ye hoo Jack Wilson en us injoyed oorsels. We went te
see Peter Cassidy in the Club en we were varry kindly treat. We had
two small ports a peece, en a draw e th' pipe; en Aa sais te Jack, "Wat
dis th' think if we hev e trip te th' seaside?" He sais, "Aal reet." So we
teuk th' tram in the Street for e lang ride is we thowt, but we hadint
gone far till th' tram stopt en Jacky en me sat still. We nivvor knaws te
she starts te cum back ower aguain, en teuk es back te th' Markit, but
it cost tuppince each wae. But aal bairns likes e ride.

If ye hevint been et Sheels laitly, ye'll see a big change wen ye de
gan. Ye'll find th' seaside in th' Markit Plaice. That's th' proper plaice
for'd. Luk oot next week for th' trip freh Tantoby Club to Jarrow
Excelsior Club.

A PICTURE HALL AT TANTOBIE

The Star Picture Hall was the Hall of the Tantobie Co-operative Society Store and seated 550 people. It was opened in September 1911 with the Co-operative Society as the Licensee. In 1920, Mr David Kelly became the Licensee, followed by Mr J.H. Fisher in 1922 and he held the Licence until the picture hall closed on 11th May 1929[6].

The Star Picture Hall, as well as showing films, had live performances from singers, comedians, musicians and others during the film interlude.

Tommy Armstrong wrote this poem in praise of 'The Star' and apart from it having been in the local newspaper in 1913[7], there is no trace of it having been published elsewhere. That same year, the management provided a benefit concert at The Star in aid of Tommy Armstrong who by that time had suffered from strokes[7].

Auve been in lots o' pictor halls at Stanla an' Sooth Moor,
At Annfield Plain an' Dipton, that please both rich and poor;
Aw winnit try te run thim doon, because thor is nee caul,
But ar must say the best auve seen is at Tantobie Pictor Haull.

Tuaik my advice en cum this week, en see "The Wummin en White,"
En Maudie Vere, the dancor, fills the audience wi' delite;
Or, if ye fancy russelin, ye hey nowt te dee but caul
En meet the Russian champion in Tantobie Pictor Haull.

Aa thowt thet last week's pictors nivver could be beet;
But I suen seen the difference wen Aa went on Monday neet;
Aa nivver hord thim taak afore, nor seed thim play at ball;
But ye shud cum this week te the Tantobie Pictor Haull.

If ye've not been here afore, ye'll find it close beside the Stor';
Ye'll see a crood aboot the door at the Pictor Haull, Tantobie;
This haul is crooded ivery neet, te yung an' awd it is a treet,
Cum suen or ye'll not get a seet i' the Pictor Haull, Tantobie.

Tantobie Co-operative Store.

THE PRUDENT PITMAN

In 1913, the local newspaper published the first part of this poem from Tommy Armstrong[8]. The last two lines of the poem stated that Tommy would be writing more on the subject the following week. True to his word, the second part of the poem was in the newspaper the following week[9]. Tommy did not give a title to the poem but the content makes it appropriate to be called 'The Prudent Pitman'.

It is of interest that the cost of all the items referred to by Tommy and his expenditure, did work out at fourpence three-farthings per day. So, in spite of suffering with the after effects of a stroke, which wasn't his first, Tommy wrote this very entertaining poem and made sure the mathematics in it would stand up to any future audit.

Apart from the two dates on which the poem was found in the newspapers, there is no trace of it having been published elsewhere, either before or since those dates.

The Stanley News – Thursday February 27th 1913

MR. THOS. ARMSTRONG, POET

I've been thinking just lately of joining the Store.
You will say I am right when I tell you what for:
The checks every quarter will do me some good.
It will help to supply me with clothing and food:
When I tell you my income, and which way it goes,
You'll say there's no wonder I wear shabby clothes.
Nine and seven pence a fortnight I get for my pay,
My food comes to fourpence three-farthings a day.

Four shillings for lodgings which I freely give,
Which leaves five and sevenpence on which I must live:
And when I have paid for my groceries and bed,
You'll say I'm fresh looking the way I am fed:
I cannot buy beef, pork, mutton or ham,
My through-the-week dinner is treacle or jam;
Believe me or not, it's true what I say,
I'm living on fourpence three-farthings a day.

There's plenty of people around us, I know,
Who like to jump over a dyke where it's low:
There's some people says that I'm often in pubs,
Some says I back horses and frequent the Clubs:
Because I'm afflicted I must be confined,
I meet with some people both feeling and kind:
For drink I've no money to squander away,
I've only got fourpence three-farthings a day.

I used to back horses in days that's gone by,
That is quite true, which I will not deny:
To the pubs and the clubs I go, it is true,
Where can I go when I've nothing to do?
I'm in a club now while writing this poem,
Drinking hop bitters, and I feel quite at home:
If you fancy my cavil, you only need say,
And live upon fourpence three-farthings a day.

Since my affliction it takes a long time
For me to compose and write out a rhyme:
If I live till next week, I will try to amuse
Every reader that takes 'The West Stanley News'.
I will finish my poem, and go home for my tea,
I know that a kipper is waiting for me:
Next week you will hear what I've got to say
About living on fourpence three-farthings a day.

The Stanley News – Thursday March 6th 1913

TOMMY ARMSTRONG, PITMAN POET

My poem in last week, and this one today,
Are both on living on such a small pay:
Don't think I am asking assistance from you,
I hope that I never will have it to do.
I am writing because I have nothing to do,
Yet still all I say is perfectly true:
The next commences to show you the way
How to live on fourpence three-farthings a day.

One shilling for butter, and sixpence for jam:
I cannot be bothered with bacon or ham:
There's one tin of treacle at sixpence a tin,
I have to be careful, and put it on thin:
Ninepence a fortnight I pay for corned beef,
This saves me from asking for parish relief;
Fivepence for sugar a fortnight I pay,
Out of my fourpence three-farthings a day.

There's sixpence for milk, and eightpence for tea,
With my tea-caddy I dare not make free:
Fourpence for baccy, I do like a pull,
It cheers a man up, sometimes when he's dull:
Twopence for kippers, and ninepence for bread,
It costs five and sevenpence for me to be fed:
Reckon my bill up, and then you will say
I'm living on fourpence three-farthings a day.

After this week I'm done with all foods,
Because I'm in want of some drapery goods:
It is the ambition of woman and man
To keep themselves clean if they possibly can:
You can wear stockings until they want darning,
Then they want footing with worsted or yarn:
Mine will go holey, that's all I can say,
I've only got fourpence three-farthings a day.

I have no desire to be handsomely dressed,
I only want trousers, a jacket and vest:
And if I don't get them, I'll never lose heart,
I'll get one to serve me when life does depart:
I'm not in a hurry, but this we all know,
We cannot tell when, but we all have to go:
There is one thing I know, when I do go away,
I'll get more than fourpence three-farthings a day.

I know I've lived longer that what was expected,
I offered to die, but it was not accepted:
Before being afflicted, I could give a joke,
I wish I had gone when I met with this stroke:
I will now conclude and finish by saying
I'm in Tantobie Club, and the piano is playing:
I'm drinking hop bitters both happy and gay,
And living on fourpence three-farthings a day.

Fourpence three-farthings on which Tommy was living each day.

THE SUMMER FLIES

This is a funny poem, written by Tommy Armstrong, about the nuisance flies can be. It was first found in the local newspaper in 1913[10] then again in 1918[11]. There is no trace of it having been published elsewhere.

Oh little fly, how can you try, to rob me of my sleep;
You little things, with legs and wings, go somewhere else to creep;
You tickle so, you may not know, yet still I cannot find
It in my heart, with you to start or be to you unkind.

When I'm in bed, on my bald head, you jump about and play,
And if I shift, you are so swift, you quickly flyaway.
When I'm in first, you're always worst, I've noticed in the past,
But if I could, I'm sure I would, catch you and make you fast.

I sometimes think for a skating rink, my head must have been made
Because with me you make so free, and never seem afraid.
But I will watch, and if I catch, one of you or more,
Every fly will have to die, like those that's gone before.

You little flies, you are no size, yet still you can do harm;
You flock together, when the weather, puts in nice and warm.
You sport and play, while it is day, as long as it is light;
It seems to me you cannot see, when it is dark at night.

You so increase, there is no peace, no matter where I be,
On stool or chair, you will be there, you like tormenting me.
The treacle tin, when you get in, where you've not been before
Your days are past, you stick so fast, you'll fly about no more.

On crumbs of bread, you oft are fed, or anything that's sweet
The sugar pot, keep out you'll not, to you it is a treat.
Nestle's tin, that has milk in, when it is open wide,
To turn my back, to have a crack, I find some flies inside.

When I'm at tea, 'tis there you'll be, no matter what I do,
In the cup, from which I sup, I often meet with you.
You silly fly, 'tis there you die, by getting in hot tea;
If you keep out, there is no doubt, you still would trouble me.

It can be seen where you have been, in day-light or in dark,
On picture frame, the glass the same, you always leave your mark;
Wherever you are, if there's a jar, if it is full of fat,
You will be there, to have a share, but you stick fast in that.

If I kill one, when it is gone, there's twenty in its place,
You seem to know, that I'm your foe, you dance about my face.
So keep off me, wherever I be, go somewhere else to dance;
For every fly, will have to die, if you give me a chance.

You little pests, we only rest when all the lights are out;
You cannot see, to make so free, you cease to fly about;
But in the morn, you do return, as soon as it is light,
You sport and play, another day until it is dark at night.

In Summer time, you are sublime, but when it puts in cold,
Your sporting days, and dirty ways are done with young and old.
We will rejoice, all in one voice, when you have gone from here,
We'll sing and say: "Oh Happy Day", we have no flies to fear.

TOMMY ARMSTRONG,
1 Oak Terrace, Tantobie, S.O.
Pitman Poet

These flies would certainly have added to Tommy's torment!

TANTOBIE WEDNESDAY FOOTBALL TEAM

This poem by Tommy Armstrong praises the prowess of the football team in its first season of existence. Whether the poem is based on fact or is one of Tommy's improvisations is not known.

It was found in the local newspaper in 1913[12] but no trace can be found of it having been published elsewhere, either prior to or since that date

I am not a football player yet I go to see them play,
I've seen some scientific games at home, likewise away.
I've often see Newcastle play and Sunderland as well,
How many League and Cup-tie games I've seen I cannot tell.
I've often stood and watched them play until I was wet through,
Yet I was quite delighted to see what they could do.
Other times I've trembled when snow did heavily fall,
I often used to wonder how the players could see the ball.

But now I need not go so far to see a first class game,
Tantobie has got up a team which soon will have a name.
This is their first season but if you saw them on,
You would think they had been playing in seasons that have gone.
Since they have commenced to play, I'll tell you what they've done,
How many other teams they've played and what they've lost and won.
They've played eight games since they began, up to the present day,
Four games at Tantobie and the other four away.

Their first game was at Consett, were they were beat by one,
Tantobie men were satisfied, for all they had got none.
A short time passed until they met to play their second game,
Consett thought they could not lose, Tantobie thought the same.
Because they beat Tantobie team by one the game before,
Tantobie showed them how to play, they never let them score.
The Wednesday's team won quite easily and when the game was done,
The referee declared the game – Tantobie four to one.

They played a draw with Chopwell, a draw with Annfield Plain,
But they will find a different team if they should meet again.
Each man is young and active and always on the move,
Their motto is to play each game in harmony and love.
And they are so improving, no matter where they play,
In pleasure and enjoyment, they spend their half a day.
They've played two draws, lost two games and four games they have won,
We hope to see them win the League before the season's done.

Front Street, Tantobie.

They won the last four games they played, seventeen to none,
I think they'll see the Palace yet if they keep going on.
The only practice which they get is when they go to play,
That is on the Wednesday when they have half a day.
No one in the neighbourhood would ever think or dream,
That the Tantobie Wednesday's could bring out such a team.
With hand on heart they have agreed never to give up,
Until they go to London and bring away the Cup.

Before I finish up my poem I will tell you each man's name,
Then you will say no wonder at them playing so well each game.
George Harris is goalkeeper, the best we've ever seen,
For to be a local man, no matter where we've been.
He is fearless and determined, let the ball come quick or slow,
He is always at his post, let it come high or low.
No team need try to break him down, for he will never yield,
When they expect they've got a goal the ball is down the field.

Tantobie team's goalkeeper is engaged behind a bar,
He makes all comers welcome, let then come from near or far.
At the Oak Tree, Tantobie, you'll see him every day,
Except on the Wednesdays, when he has to go and play.
The full back's Trevenna Harrison, the other is John Cox,
They work the ball between them as sly as any fox.
The half backs Jack Wilkinson, Jack Adamson and Joe Clark,
It makes no matter where they play, they are up to the mark.

The forwards Joe Ridley, Tom Oyston and Tom Smith,
They are as fine young men as a team can get in with.
Then comes James Doney and the other is Joe Reay,
In fact they are a jolly lot, no matter where they play.
When they have such directors as Charles Harris and George Shield,
They should never lose a match when they go on the field.
There's William Holmes, John Hewitson and Tom Harris too,
Each man is determined to bring the Wednesdays through.

*How a local newspaper illustrated a match in 1919 – this one is
Newcastle versus Sunderland.*

TANTOBIE WORKMEN'S CLUB
OXO BANQUET

This amusing poem was written by Tommy and what a banquet it must have been? Was it fantasy or was it written about a function that did not turn out as expected? The poem was in the local newspaper in 1913[13]:

One morning as I sat, with my feet upon the mat,
Enjoying the sweet comforts of a smoke;
A knock came to the door, I was soon upon the floor,
Yet I thought somebody was knocking for a joke;
I lifted up the sneck, I thought it was a cheque
Which the postman placed so gently in my hand.
When I opened out the note, it said, Dear Mr Poet,
We are going to have a banquet so grand.

We give you an invite to come tomorrow night
To a banquet in Tantobie Workmen's Club;
No matter where you've been, such as this you've never seen
In a chapel or a hall or a pub.
You can easily contrive to be at the Club at five
So I made up my mind for to go;
I was very pleased I went, for a merry night I spent
At the banquet of biscuits and Oxo.

When each man got his seat, it was a perfect treat,
For Oxo was flying all around;
No carving knife or fork, nor mutton, beef or pork,
There was nothing but the spoons to be found;
Each man had a cup, from which he had to sup,
Each table had a cloth on white as snow;
When each man was in his place, the steward said the grace,
At the banquet of biscuits and Oxo.

There was biscuits in galore, I counted thirteen score,
And fifty cups of Oxo was gone;
The waiters were all glad, there was no more to be had,
The Oxo and the biscuits were done;
There was one man broke a cup, the steward says, "What's up?
To do a trick like that sets you low;
If you have got tight since you came in here tonight,
You have only had biscuits and Oxo."

When all was cleared away, a few words from Mr Gray,
Thanking both the steward and the stewardess.
He said, "I'll not forget the way we have been treat,"
He spoke up to the mark we must confess;
That is all I've got to say until a week today,
To each reader that takes 'The Stanley News',
I will try to let you know about the banquet of Oxo,
Because I know it will each one amuse.

TOMMY THE POET SIGNED ON

This humorous poem was written by Tommy Armstrong, then aged 66 years, as if he was 'signing on' to fight in the First World War. It was found in the local newspaper in 1914[14]:

Right: A cartoon of a recruiting sergeant.

Since this present war began in thousands men have gone,
To fight for King and Country and I've signed my name as one.
I went by bus to Stanley town the other Monday night,
The choice of ways was open, it was either starve or fight.

I knew that I was tall enough, and forty round the chest,
But whether I'd be passed or not – well, doctor he'd know best.
If all goes well a few days hence, they'll tell me "Yes" or "No",
I'm ready now at any time, just want the word to go.

The gentleman I went to see gave ear to my request,
And said they'd do what'er they could to list me with the rest.
I thanked them then and took my leave, I'm waiting now the word,
To shoulder arms and step right out to meet the German herd.

If we should meet on Monday next – and I expect we will,
I hope they'll say I'm just the man a little gap to fill.
And if I do not write to you, be sure that I have gone;
The Kaiser is as good as dead when Tommy gets signed on.

The new recruits I often see, and often hear them say,
They've plenty food to eat, and get, likewise, a bob a day.
Why! I have only fourpence – that's dividing their's by three,
And whilst I've other reasons that is good enough for me.

I have for years been on parade and never lost a day,
I'm well trained, fit and well what more could true men wish to say?
So when you hear that I have gone, whilst you sit at your door,
Just smoke your pipe and think at ease, that Tommy's stopped the war.

THE TRIP FROM TANTOBIE UNION CLUB TO JARROW EXCELSIOR CLUB

This poem and story about the above trip was in four parts. It explains the trip in some detail and some of the funny activities that took place. It was written by Tommy Armstrong and the four parts appeared in four separate issues of the local newspaper in 1913[15].

Apart from appearing in those newspapers, no trace can be found of any of the parts having been published elsewhere.

On the sixth of September, I very well remember,
It was on a fine summer's day.
Thirty young men (all alive) agreed to have a drive,
And where to meet before they set away.
A young man said to me, "I would like to see you go with us,
And I will stand a treat."
'Twas him that paid my fare, or I would not have been there,
Then it was lucky for to get a seat.

George Humphrey's two brakes, which very often takes,
All the people that desire to go.
Down to Whitley or Shields, or any way,
If vacant he will never say no.
So shortly after ten, he came to seek his men,
We all got in as soon as he did stop.
There were twenty six inside, as many as could ride,
And four upon the 'dicky' on the top.

We made up our minds that day before we went away,
That we wouldn't call at any pub.
But there would be a stop for each to get a drop
When we got as far as Whickham Club.
The company on the whole had a fancy button hole,
They got them in the Club when they met.
All colours could be seen, yellow, pink and green,
Such a class as them are hard to get.

As we went down the street we could hear the horses feet,
The weather being so fine, the roads were dry.
The women folk did stand and kept waving up their hands,
At each side of the road as we passed by.
We went through Clough Dene, where gardens could be seen,
Each man could have a pleasant look.
We had to climb a hill, there was only one sat still,
The others walked very near to Pickering Nook.

A Brake owned by Humphreys of Tanfield Lea which could have been one actually used to transport the men to Jarrow.

As soon as they got in, the horses did begin,
To travel on the road in such a style.
You'd think they knew where they were going to,
We were soon to the far end of the mile.
We passed the Hobson Hotel, the Crookgate pub as well,
We passed the Fellside pub on our way.
If we had made a call for to see them all,
We would not have seen Jarrow Club that day.

We got to Whickham next, not a passenger was vexed,
When they knew the brakes were going to stop.
The weather was so warm, to them it was a charm,
Every man was wishing for a drop.
To the Club we went away but we hadn't long to stay,
We didn't get as much as we could take.
We had a drop or two, of course, we made it do,
Then we finished up and got the brake.

We bid them all "good-day" before we went away,
The Steward and the members that were there.
They invited one and all to be sure and give a call,
The best of kindness every man should share.
Then the drivers with their whip, just gave each horse a tip,
They started off with their load.
There was no delay the remainder of the way,
We didn't stop any more on the road.

We knew if we were there, we would have no call to care,
Everything was pleasure to the end.
In the Excelsior Club there was plenty of grub,
And every member treat us as a friend.
We landed safe and sound and the friendliness we found,
I cannot tell you in my present poem.
But I will write again and unto you explain,
And tell you all about our coming home.

Mr. Editor, – If Aad written me poem aboot wor trip freh Tantobie te Jarra an' back, it wad a taken ower much room, but Aal write shortly an' tell aal aboot hoo we enjoyed worsels at Jarra.

Two of wor members played for the championship at billiards and of course, they won; and another played thor champion at dominoes and of course, he won an' all. Aa wad hae wrote last week, but Aa've been se poorly. Anyway, luk oot for the finish o' th' trip.

TANTOBIE CLUB TRIP TO JARROW EXCELSIOR CLUB

'Tis just a week ago since I wrote to let you know,
About the merry time which we had.
From setting first away till we finished up the day,
Every man said he did feel glad.
That day we did arrive, the Club was all alive,
The President and Secretary too;
Gave each man a shake as we left the brake,
More kindness before I never knew.

Into the Club we went where a jolly time was spent,
At billiards a few men went in to play.
And many other games but I could not tell their names,
Were played at to pass the time away.
The Steward was so free, it was not hard to see,
The Stewardess was smiling all the day.
The reception which we had made us all feel glad,
From going there until we came away.

The President came in, to invite he did begin,
He said, "Tantobie men come this way.
Onlookers and you players, are invited up the stairs,
To partake of what there is prepared today."
We put the games to rest and granted his request,
Until we had come down the stairs again.
The tables were so set that I never shall forget,
As long as ever memory does remain.

When each man took his place, the Chairman he said grace,
The waiters then began to do their work.
There was mutton, beef and tongue to suit both old and young,
Boiled ham and splendid roasted pork.
Our wants were all supplied, each man being satisfied,
Down into the billiard room we came.
I heard Ted Watkins say, "Robert Atthey and John Gray,
With two Jarrow men were going to have a game."

The champions from the west, to see who was the best,
All comers they are open for to play.
William Walker and his marrow, the champions of Jarrow,
We could see they were losing all the way.
And when the game was done, Tantobie men had won,
I heard the two Jarrow men say;
"We have not played before, and we'll play with them no more,
With Robert Atthey and John Gray."

Another man of fame, Eli Rounsley is his name,
He's an expert player at dominoes.
He began to play with another man that day,
The champion of Jarrow I suppose.
They hadn't been long on when the game was two to one,
Many thought the Jarrow man would win.
When the game was through, Eli was five to two,
The Jarrow man said he would give in.

Tantobie Co-operative Store Horse & Cart. Could this have been used in the absence of the second brake of Humphreys?

When the driver's went to yoke, we sat and had a smoke,
And talked about the pleasures of the day.
Telling where we'd been and the pleasant sights we'd seen,
At South Shields the time they were away.
The piano then began, Sammy Thompson was the man,
That played to each singer as he sung.
Billy Walton he sung two, Harry Curry sung a few,
I never heard them sing as well before.

The brakes then did arrive, which did each man deprive,
Of hearing Harry sing us any more.
Every man was there and we quickly did prepare,
It was time for us to be upon the road.
The moon was shining bright and we bid them all good-night,
And the horses started off with their load.

(To be continued next week)

WOR JARRA TRIP

We set awae freh Jarra Club, et hauf past hite et neet,
The drivers stopt th' horses et th' cornor iv th' street,
We thowt it was th' wae we com'; but there was sumthing straing,
Th' time we 'ad been e th' Club thare'd been e rapid chaing.

We nue we com' throo Franklin Street, becaws we saw the nuaim,
We cud see th' caul'd this Estor Street, so it cudn't be the suaim.
Th' drivers thowt it was th' wae, but still thae warn't shoor,
Thare the braiks en horsis stud for nearly hauf en hoor.

Aw gat that weery wi sitten, aw wis just gan te get oot en wauk, wen aw gat me ee on a bobby stannen ecross th' street. Aw gav him e wussil en wen e com across, he sais, "Wat's rang?" Aw sais tiv him, "Mistor, we're sitten stannen in difikilties heer. We com' throo Franklin Street wen we com' th' dae, en th' caul it Estor Street noo." He sais, "Oh aw see yor straingers heer. Th' nuaims e streets e Jarra is chaing'd ivory fortnith. That is th' suaim wae oot is ye com' biv." Aw sais, "This puts me i th' mind wen aw wis et Sooth Sheels we th' awd men's trip freh th' Victoria Club. Enuther chep en me gat inte th' tram te gan te th' peer heed en then te th' seaside; en wen we gat thare, buaith th' peer heed en th' seaside wis shifted inte th' Markit Plaice. So he browt us back ower eguain for uthor tupince. If ye went inte the' Markit for a haporth e fish, ye gat wet shod; but aw wis vary plees'd te see th' Markit drie th' dae and th' seaside back tiv its awd plaice." So aw put me hand e mi pockit en aw gav th' bobby e penny. He seem'd te be plees'd wi'd. Aw wud e geen him tupince, but aw nue hees pae wis gannen on. We'll meet eguain.

Jack Atty bloo hees wussil, en the drivers set awae,
Bob Broon 'ad bowt e orgin, witch he seun began te plae.
Th' horsis seem'd te knaw th' teun, thae went in such a stile,
En wen he sau it suited them, he plaid for mony e mile.

We nivvor cauld ipon th' road freh leevin Jarra Club,
Te we gat te Hebron Nue Toon, then we stopt beside e pub.
Sum went in te hev a drop, en uthors did sit still,
Te watch th' horsis es thae stud yet eech man gat hees gill.

Auve been awae for e fortnith. Aw heard thit Dublin en Ireland wis
gannen te fite, so aw thowt aw wad trie to muaik peece. En wen aw
wis up yem, aw wad see thit we did get Hoam Rool. We hev e reet
for'd. Auve ad e queer time ont wi Carsin en e few e th' biggins, bu awl
not let it rest thare. Luck oot shortly for th' finish e th' trip.

The famous shipyard cranes in Jarrow.

JARRA TRIP

To finish the trip from Tantobie to Jarrow, from Jarrow back over again.
The pleasures and troubles we had on the way, to you I will try to
explain.
At Hebburn New Town we called on our way, it was the first and the
last,
Whenever we meet with people we know, time seems to travel too fast.

While they took refreshments I sat in the brake, one, then another
would come.
They all came to ask me what I would take, a lemon dash, whiskey or
rum.
Some of them know that I never drink ale and liquors I always detest,
Port wine is the strongest that ever I drink, I find that it suits me the
best.

When they were ready we set off again, the singing and dancing began,
One man was ready to stand up and sing as soon as the other was
done.
All went well till we got to the Fellside but when between there and
Crookgate,
The singing and dancing was done for the night, the reason I'll try to
relate.

Like a shot from a gun the tyre flew off on to the road with a clatter,
Each man left his seat, the driver likewise, and soon they saw what
was the matter.
When they saw the tyre had come off the wheel, to each other they
started to talk,
When the driver said, "Men, I am sorry to say to you, everyone must
walk."

Mistor Editor, – Thae nue aw cudint wauk. Aw wis lifted on te th'
dicky beside th' drivor. Aw wis aul reet. Thare wis one e wor cheps
soond esleep e th' braik. Thae waikint im up en telt him he had te
wauk. Esteed e getten oot e th' braik like th' rest, he tummild oot. He
gat oot sharpor than he wanted, en wen he wis axt if he wis ony warse,
he said, "No." But wen he put his hand tiv his inside pockit, he sais,
"Au've getten a bad bat te this side. Au've smashed a gill e rum aul te
bits, en spill'd th' bottil." Thae set off te wauk bu Aw stuck te th' dicky.
Aw gat inte th' tuthor braik et th' top e Cruckgait Bank. We lended
suaifly yem.

TOMMY AIRMSTRANG
Pitman Poet, Tantoby.

PART SIX

The Works of
William Hunter Armstrong

Authors of some books and old residents of Tanfield Lea have said that WHA wrote some poems and he was popularly known as 'Poety'[1,2&3]. In spite of considerable research, including old newspapers, only three of his works have been found. If he did compose any more, like Tommy's, they are probably lost forever.

THE COURAGE OF HENRY POLGLASE

This poem by WHA was not given a title by him so based on the content, the above title seems appropriate.

It relates to an incident in May 1942 when Henry Polglase and George Brown were underground in Tanfield Lea Colliery. There was a large fall of coal from the roof of the seam which partly buried Brown who was in danger of suffocating. Polglase had no use in his left leg and thought it was pinned but another effort to drag it free made him realise it was broken. Seeing how Brown was trapped and realising help was needed, Polglase, despite the danger of further falls, crawled 35 yards over fallen timber and other obstructions to summon assistance. When people answered his calls, Polglase told them, "Never mind me, get the other fellow out. There is a great weight of coal on his back and he is in danger of choking." Brown later said that but for the action of Polglase, he would not have survived. In February 1943, Polglase was presented with a framed certificate and a cheque for £20 from the Carnegie Hero Fund Trust, plus other monies from Unions and public subscriptions[4].

As a result of this presentation being reported in the local newspaper, WHA submitted a poem but the newspaper only published part of it in an article the following week[5]. The article reads as follows but no trace can be found of the missing verses to which the article refers:

Mr Armstrong's Tribute To Mine Hero

"We cannot reproduce the whole of the poem, which contains an eloquent tribute to Mr Polglase but give some of the verses."

> In the annals of history many true stories are told
> Of heroes and heroines whose names are enrolled,
> But in life's experience you'll find none more bold
> Than the Miners.
>
> As usual they travel to their work every day,
> Optimistic and cheerful, with not the best pay;
> Unselfish, courageous – but that is their way
> The Miners.
>
> In this demonstration we meet here tonight,
> To honour a comrade who was in a sad plight;
> With courage undaunted, thinking not of his life
> Henry Polglase.

The verses continue to describe how Mr Polglase and Wm. Brown were caught by a roof fall and how Henry wriggled himself free and though badly injured and without light, crawled some distance to find a rescuer.

> Can you imagine this man, hurt more than his mate,
> Creeping and trailing, heedless of his fate.
> Forty yards or more, yes and in such a state
> Henry Polglase.

The verses continue to refer to the self sacrifice of the workers and concluded.

> To all the mineworkers our nation should show
> Respect and fair dealing both at bank and below.
> For they get the coals which such blessings bestow
> On Mankind

The opening of Tanfield Lea Colliery Welfare.

A DAY OF REJOICING
NATIONALISATION OF THE MINES

This poem by William Hunter Armstrong was found amongst the working papers of the Folklorist, A L Lloyd but does not appear to have been published anywhere[6].

In 1945, as the war came to an end, the Government announced its intention to nationalise coal mining, and the Coal Industry Nationalisation Act 1946 provided for the nationalisation of the entire industry. The National Coal Board was established and was given sole responsibility for managing and running the industry. W.H. Armstrong clearly wrote this poem to celebrate the Government announcement in 1945.

A year to be remembered is nineteen forty five,
When the people of this country proved they were still alive.
They elected a Labour Government their wishes to fulfil
And they started off as one, and are hard at it still.

We're celebrating now the passing of nationalisation
Of the mines, which will prove a blessing to the nation.
Too long they have been run by and for the Profiteers
Who have bleeded the miners for over a hundred years.

Thanks to our pioneers who in the years that's past
Toiled hard, had visions which are fulfilled at last,
Keir Hardie, Smiley and others, who with courage paved the way
And have made many things possible that we enjoy today.

This a day of rejoicing, Nationalisation of the Mines,
If all men do their best the future holds better times.
With pride each one can say, the mines belong to me
So I will do my best to make it as it should be.

There is one thing to remember, Workmen and Officials too,
We're all workmen for the nation and that is something new.
So let's all pull together and very soon we'll see,
The flag that means the target, flying at Tanfield Lea.

Tanfield Lea Colliery was sunk in eighteen twenty nine,
A hundred and eighteen years ago so it's an oldish mine.
In eighteen forty seven the Joiceys bought it out,
And their profits were enormous, of that there is no doubt.

Now we're left with thin seams, still a profit can be made,
By trust and co-operation and if men are better paid.
A better set of workmen in the county can't be found,
Than those at Tanfield Lea Colliery who are working underground.

A plea for better airway is something overdue
And certainly the tub way should be well kept too.
The ponies should be thought of and seen to get their rest,
They're part of the scheme and need to do their best.

Hats off to Mr Shinwell and the Labour Government as well,
With all the opposition, their souls they would not sell.
The National Coal Board appointed and all doing what they can,
Success is sure to come to the Nationalisation Plan.

Crowds flocked to pits throughout County Durham on Vesting Day –
1st January 1947. Here local people gather around Murton Colliery to
witness the start of 'the new era' for miners.

FAREWELL TO COLLIERY OWNERS

This is clearly a follow-up to the poem of William Hunter Armstrong – 'A DAY OF REJOICING – NATIONALISATION OF THE MINES'. This poem coincided with and celebrated the start of managing and running the mining industry by the National Coal Board known as 'Vesting Day' on the 1st January 1947.

The poem was published in a book of works by the Folklorist, A.L. Lloyd[7].

Right: William Hunter Armstrong standing in front of the Tanfield Lea Lodge Banner of the National Union of Mineworkers on Vesting Day – 1st January 1947.

For three hundred years or more you have owned the mines,
And all throughout those years, the miners had bad times.
You never cared, loved far away, the managers were your tools,
To make for you your profits, and acted more like fools.

Unlike the men, your nest is feathered. You do not need the dole.
But if justice reigned, you should now go down and hew the coal.
Your notices have expired now; of that we're very glad,
But of all men in the country, you'll be miserable and sad.

Farewell you owners, we're sorry you haven't gone before.
You did much damage to our homes, and now you can't do more.
Farewell, farewell, the time has come, the sentence on you will be
'Inasmuch as you did it to the least ye did it unto me.'

I'm unfurling the flag today for the NCB and state,
And hope everyone will do their best, as the scheme they undertake.
Be present every working day, that is if well and fit;
Then we shall hear the target fixed being reached at every pit.

FAMILY TREE – PARENTS, SIBLINGS & SOME DESCENDANTS OF TOMMY ARMSTRONG

LEGEND: b Born c Circa m Married d Died

Timothy ARMSTRONG b.23.04.1815 d.21.02.1871	m 22.05.1842	Mary WILSON b.27.09.1820 d.23.10.1883	**Other Children of Timothy & Mary ARMSTRONG** William Wilson b.04.12.1843 d.01.12.1891 Henry b.12.03.1851 d.25.10.1924 Mary Alice b.30.05.1855 d.15.10.1884 Timothy b.05.03.1858 d.23.12.1916

|

Thomas ARMSTRONG b.15.08.1848 d.30.08.1920	m 25.12.1869	Mary Ann HUNTER b.30.05.1853 d.03.04.1898	

|

Other Children of Tommy & Mary Ann ARMSTRONG

William Hunter
ARMSTRONG
b.27.12.1874
d.18.04.1953

Mary b.24.05.1871 d.29.10.1944
Margaret b.24.11.1872 d.23.10.1873
Jane b.12.01.1874 d.17.03.1874
Timothy b.06.02.1878 d.24.04.1884
Ada Jane b.07.04.1881 d.28.07.1881
Thomas Henry b. 21.08.1882
d.16.10.1956
George Hunter b. 04.03.1885
d. 06.10.1885
Peter b. 25.01.1887 d. 02.06.1973
Margaret b. 28.02.1888 d. 27.11.1979
Barbara Alice b.19.07.1890
d. 22.06.1906
Hannah Jane b. 22.08.1891
d. 04.08.1917
Timothy b. 04.08.1894 d. 13.02.1896
Sarah Jane b. 16.02.1896
d. 06.02.1897

|

1st Marriage: 14.03.1896
Elizabeth ROBSON b.17.08.1875
Divorced: 12.07.1909

Children: Nora Hunter b.21.02.1898
d.22.03.1927
James b.28.02.1901 d.21.02.1986

|

2nd Marriage: 09.03.1910
Annie LIGHTFOOT b. c.1866 d.04.06.1941

No children of this marriage

|

Relationship c. 1930 to 1934
With Margaret Annie Eliza TILLY
b.17.02.1901 d.11.07.1977

Produced: Raymond Wilfred TILLY
b.26.08.1934

|

3rd Marriage: 09.05.1942
Agnes MOIR
b.05.07.1902 d.05.11.1988

Child: Norman ARMSTRONG
b.07.08.1942 d.13.08.1942

GLOSSARY

Some of the words and terms which are to be found in a number of Tommy Armstrong's poems and correspondence with newspaper editors.

AAa	I
aad, aud	old
aal	all
aa'll	I will
aan	own
aa's	I am
aboot	about
aflaid	afraid
agyen	again
airm	arm
alang	along
bairn	child
bait	packed lunch
bank	the surface
bigins	big ones
bord	bird or board
borst	burst
botil en box	water bottle & lunch box
Boyd and Elliot	Oarsmen of the time
braikemin	brakesman in charge of winding engine at pit
buain	bone
byeuts	boots
caad	cold
caal	call
caiges	cages
cavil	work station allocated by lot
claes	clothes
cockt	cocked
County Avorage	Average 'piece rate' in the County
coup me creels	turn a summersault
crood	crowd
cutten fuaices	cut faces
dabin	bumping
de	do
deed	dead
dis	does
dorty	dirty
drucken	drunken
Ducks en Savolois	Meat Savouries

eftor	after
eneuf	enough
faal	fall
falde to deed	frightened to death
fethor	father
fettiled	mended
flaid	afraid
flat	area of work in the mine
fore shift	early shift
for fairs	fairly
frae	from
fuaices	faces
galewae	pit pony
gan	go
gob	mouth
haad	hold
heed	head
hev	have
hind	herdsman
horsel	herself
inte	into
ivory	every
Keeker	Surface Foreman at pit
knaa	to know
lang	long
lee	lie
lugs	ears
ma	my
mair	more
maistors	masters
marras	workmates
mesel	myself
mony	many
muthor	mother
myek	make
neb	nose
neet	night
nivvor	never
nowt	nothing
nuaim	name

oot	out
ower	over
Owerseeor	Overseer
owt	anything
Parlour end	Select part of public house where men would take women
Pollis	Policeman
potted heed	jellied meat dish
powl	pole
proggle	prickle
Pumpor	Pump Operator
raa	row of houses
ramble awd band	stony content of coal seam
reet	right
roondy coals	large lumps of coal
sair	sore
sais	says
sang	song
sark	vest
screen	where stone was separated from coal
se	so
shifters	workmen
skeets	runners up side of shaft for cages
Skeul Bordman	School Board Truant Officer
slaa	slow
sneck	gate/door latch
Store	Co-operative Society
taal	tall
te	to
thoo	thou
thor's	there is
thraa	throw
toon	town
tyek	take
varry	very
waal	wall
wad	would
warse	worse
watter	water
weel	well
Weimin	Weighman
wey	why

what fettle	how are you
whee	who
winning headways	making new inroads into the coal
witeybairn	heavy child
wivoot	without
wor	our
working wet	wet workplace at the coal face
yem	home
yen	one
yor	your
yorsel	yourself

Young lads ready to go down a Durham pit.

ADDITIONAL NOTE

The beer 'Tommy's Canny Kyebil' produced by The Stables micro brewery (featured on page 52) gives us a further word for our glossary. The word 'Kyebil' is believed to be a South Shields spelling of the word cavil – 'work station allocated by lot'.

REFERENCES

Chapter 1: Who Was Tommy

1. 'The Consett and Stanley Chronicle' dated 2nd March 1917, Page 3.
2. Census taken on the night of 30th/31st March 1851.
3. Hamsterley Parish Register entry shows the birth of Timothy Armstrong as 23rd April 1815.
4. Wigton Parish Register entry shows the baptism of Mary Wilson as 18th February 1821.
5. The Certificate shows Timothy Armstrong & Mary Wilson, both of Haswell married at Easington 22nd May 1842.
6. The Factory Act 1833 and Elementary Education Act 1870.
7. An interview with William Hunter Armstrong by Michael Dodd in 1951, a written record of which is held at Beamish Museum Resource Centre.
8. 'County Chronicle' dated 28th May 1914, Page 3.
9. 'The Story of West Stanley' by Frederick J. Wade, December 1956, Page 56.
10. 'Stanley News' dated 2nd September 1920, Page 3.
11. Durham Record Office, Reference: NCB 1/SC 109/14-19.
12. 'The Miners of Northumberland and Durham' by Richard Fynes 1873.
13. Census taken the night of 2nd/3rd April 1911 for 15 James Street, Tanfield Lea.
14. Census taken the night of 2nd/3rd April 1911 for 36 Grange Terrace, Pelton Fell.
15. Death Certificate of Ann Armstrong, 23rd November 1918 at Red Rose Cottage, Chester-le-Street.
16. 'Stanley News and Consett Chronicle' dated 30th October, Page 5; 6th November, Page 8 and 13th November 1924, Page 8.
17. 'Stanley News and Consett Chronicle' dated 6th November 1924, Page 8.

Chapter 2: The Poet

1. 'The Consett and Stanley Chronicle' dated 10th March 1916, Page 8.
2. 'The Consett and Stanley Chronicle' dated 24th March 1916, Page 4.
3. 'The Consett Guardian' dated 11th December 1869, Page 2.
4. Notes by A.L. Lloyd, Folklorist of an interview with William Hunter Armstrong which are held with numerous papers of Lloyd in the Special Collections at Goldsmiths College, New Cross – part of London University. Ref. Code: GB2603 Lloyd.
5. 'Das Leben Eines Englischen Bergarbeitersangers' in Deutsches Jahrbuch fur Volkskunde, 1964, Band 10, Teil 1, pages 133-143.
6. 'The Consett Guardian' dated 8th February 1873, Page 5 and Death Certificate dated 13th April 1874.
7. 'The Consett Guardian' dated 22nd March 1878, Page 5 and Death Certificate dated 16th December 1877.

8. 'The Consett Guardian' dated 16th January 1880, Page 5.

9. 'Consett Chronicle' dated 1st February 1901, Page 3.

10. 'Consett Chronicle' dated 4th January 1901, Page 5.

11. 'The Consett and Stanley Chronicle' dated 24th March 1916, Page 4.

12. An interview with William Hunter Armstrong by Michael Dodd in 1951, a written record of which is held at Beamish Museum Resource Centre.

Chapter 3: Move to Whitley Bay

1. 'Consett Chronicle' dated 21st February 1902, Page 5.

2. 'Consett Chronicle' dated 7th March 1902, Page 5.

3. 'Consett Chronicle' dated 23rd May 1902, Page 7.

4. Various Internet Web-sites.

5. Various Internet Web-sites.

6. 'Consett Chronicle' dated 26th September 1902, Page 7.

Chapter 4: Ailing Health and His Death

1. 'Consett Chronicle' dated 7th July 1899, Page 3.

2. 'The Stanley News' dated 20th March 1913, Page 3.

3. 'The Stanley News' dated 10th April 1913, Page 8 and 17th April 1913, Page 6.

4. 'County Chronicle' dated 28th May 1914, Page 3.

5. 'The Consett and Stanley Chronicle' dated 24th March 1916, Page 4.

6. 'Stanley News and Consett Chronicle' dated 14th February 1924, Page 5.

7. 'Stanley News and Consett Chronicle' dated 26th June 1924, Page 6.

8. 'Stanley News and Consett Chronicle' dated 6th November 1924, Page 4.

Chapter 6: The Character and Alleged Drunkard

1. An interview with William Hunter Armstrong by Michael Dodd in 1951, a written record of which is held at Beamish Museum Resource Centre.

2. Notes by A.L. Lloyd, Folklorist of an interview with William Hunter Armstrong which are held with numerous papers of Lloyd in the Special Collections at Goldsmiths College, New Cross – part of London University. Ref. Code: GB2603 Lloyd.

3. Transactions of the Tyneside Naturalists Club, 1863-4, Vol. VI, Page 200.

Chapter 7: Controversies

1. 'The Consett and Stanley Chronicle' dated 24th March 1916, Page 4.

2. Durham Record Office, Reference: NCB 1/SC 109/14-19.

3. Police General Order Book refers to Police Officers at Blaydon Police Station from 1864 to 1870 – Durham Record Office, Reference CCP 1/2.

4. 'The Consett Guardian' dated 1st March 1878, Page 2.

5. An interview with William Hunter Armstrong by Michael Dodd in 1951, a written record of which is held at Beamish Museum Resource Centre.

6. Notes by A.L. Lloyd, Folklorist of an interview with William Hunter Armstrong which are held with numerous papers of Lloyd in the Special Collections at Goldsmiths College, New Cross – part of London University. Ref. Code: GB2603 Lloyd.

7. 'Come all ye bold miners'. Ballads & songs of the Coalfields. Compiled by A.L. Lloyd and published in 1952, Page 138.

Chapter 8: Remembering Tommy

1. 'Newcastle Evening Chronicle' dated 9th August 1986, Page 3.

Chapter 9: Birth, Education, Three Marriages and One Divorce

1. 'Consett Chronicle' dated 28th July 1905, Page 2.

2. 'The Consett Guardian' dated 16th July 1909, Page 3 and 'Consett Chronicle' dated 23rd July 1909, Page 6.

Chapter 10: Anecdotes

1. 'Stanley News' dated 8th June 1939, Page 5

Chapter 11: Work, Union and Welfare Activities

1. 'Stanley News' dated 30th April 1953, Page 4.

2. Durham Record Office, Reference: NCB I/CO 335.

3. 'Stanley News' dated 17th November 1938, Page 7.

4. 'General History of Tanfield Lea and Neighbourhood' by the Tanfield Lea Women's Institute in 1960, Page 33.

5. 'Stanley News and Consett Chronicle' dated 29th January 1931, Page 2.

6. 'Stanley News' dated 29th August 1946, Page 4.

7. 'Stanley News' dated 5th September 1946, Page 4.

8. 'Stanley News' dated 15th April 1948, Page 4.

9. 'Stanley News' dated 26th September 1946, Page 1.

Chapter 12: The Church and Other Activities

1. 'Stanley News' dated 30th April 1953, Page 4.

2. 'Consett and Stanley Chronicle' dated 8th August 1913, Page 5.

3. Durham Record Office, Ref. No: M/Sta 126.

4. 'Jubilee History of West Stanley Co-operative Society Ltd 1876-1926' by John W. White, J.P. and Robert Simpson, F.C.R.A., Page 222.

5. Durham Record Office, Ref. No: D/DCNA 155.

6. 'Stanley News' dated 1st September 1949, Page 3.

7. Internet web-site: www.sonsoftemperance.abelgratis.co.uk

8. 'Stanley News and Consett Chronicle' dated 31st January 1924, Page 8.

9. 'Consett Chronicle' dated 15th May 1908, Page 6.

10. 'Stanley News and Consett Chronicle' dated 8th March 1923, Page 4.

11. 'The Stanley News' dated 10th March 1921, Page 2.

12. Minutes of meetings of the Newcastle upon Tyne Grand Division of the Order of the Sons of Temperance Society 1932-1953 held at Tyne & Wear Archives Service, Newcastle upon Tyne – not catalogued (2009).

Chapter 13: Relationship and Illegitimate Son

1. Personal knowledge and various church records in the possession of the author.

2. Minutes of meetings of the Newcastle upon Tyne Grand Division of the Order of the Sons of Temperance Society 1932-1953 held at Tyne & Wear Archives Service, Newcastle uponTyne – not catalogued (2009).

3. Verbal information from Betsy Hawkings (born 1915) who, as a member of the Sons of Temperance Division at Eighton Banks, used to attend meetings at Newcastle upon Tyne with Maggie Tilly and WHA.

Part Three: Thirty Previously Published Works

of Thomas Armstrong

1. 'The Consett Guardian' dated 16th January 1880, Page 2.

2. 'The Consett and Stanley Chronicle' dated 10th March 1916, Page 8.

3. 'The Story of West Stanley' by Frederick J. Wade, December 1956, Page 207.

4. 'The Times' newspaper dated 28th August 1911, Page 6.

5. An interview with William Hunter Armstrong by Michael Dodd in 1951, a written record of which is held at Beamish Museum Resource Centre and notes by A.L. Lloyd, Folklorist of an interview with William Hunter Armstrong which are held with numerous papers of Lloyd in the Special Collections at Goldsmiths College, New Cross – part of London University. Ref. Code: GB2603 Lloyd.

6. 'The Consett Guardian' dated 11th March 1892, Page 3 and subsequent weeks issues of the newspaper.

7. 'The Consett and Stanley Chronicle' dated 24th March 1916, Page 4.

8. 'The Consett Guardian' dated 25th December 1908, Page 10.

9. 'The Consett Guardian' dated 26th February 1909, Page 4.

10. 'The Consett Guardian' dated 29th January 1894, Page 3.

11. An interview with William Hunter Armstrong by Michael Dodd in 1951, a written record of which is held at Beamish Museum Resource Centre and notes by A.L. Lloyd, Folklorist of an interview with William Hunter Armstrong which are held with numerous papers of Lloyd in the Special Collections at Goldsmiths College, New Cross – part of London University. Ref. Code: GB2603 Lloyd.

12. 'The Consett Chronicle' dated 2nd August 1912, Page 8.

13. 'Consett and Stanley Chronicle' dated 6th September 1918, Page 2.

14. Notes by A.L. Lloyd, Folklorist of an interview with William Hunter Armstrong which are held with numerous papers of Lloyd in the Special Collections at Goldsmiths College, New Cross – part of London University. Ref. Code: GB2603 Lloyd.

15. 'The Consett and Stanley Chronicle' dated 24th March 1916, Page 4.
16. 'The Guardian' dated 20th November 1875, Page 3.
17. 'The Consett Guardian' dated 5th March 1886, Page 3.
18. Notes accompanying the CD 'M3M Recordings: M3MCDS1'

Part Four: Six Unpublished Works of Thomas Armstrong

1. 'The Consett and Stanley Chronicle' dated 10th March 1916, Page 8.
2. 'The Stanley News' dated 12th June 1913, Page 7.
3. 'The Stanley News' dated 26th June 1913, Page 3.
4. 'The Stanley News' dated 3rd July 1913, Page 3.
5. 'The Stanley News and North West Durham Observer' dated 18th July 1913, Page 6.

Part Five: Ten Further Unpublished Works of Thomas Armstrong

1. 'The Stanley News and North West Durham Observer' dated 1st August 1913, Page 3.
2. 'Durham Chronicle' dated 7th May 1897, Page 5 and 14th May 1897, Page 8.
3. 'Consett Chronicle' dated 11th June 1897, Page 3.
4. 'The Stanley News & North West Durham Observer' dated 29th August 1913, Page 7.
5. 'The Stanley News & North West Durham Observer' dated 19th Sep. 1913, Page 5.
6. 18th November 2009. Verbal information from Mr Frank Manders of Sunderland, a local historian specialising in cinemas and theatres.
7. 'Stanley News' dated 13th February 1913, Page 5 and 10th April 1913, Page 8.
8. 'Stanley News' dated 27th February 1913, Page 8.
9. 'Stanley News' dated 6th March 1913, Page 5.
10. 'Stanley News' dated 5th June 1913, Page 8.
11. 'Consett and Stanley Chronicle' dated 13th September 1918, Page 3.
12. 'The Stanley News & North West Durham Observer' dated 5th Dec 1913, Page 8.
13. 'The Stanley News' dated 29th May 1913, Page 7.
14. 'The Consett and Stanley Chronicle' dated 27th November 1914, Page 3.
15. 'The Stanley News & North West Durham Observer dated 3rd October 1913, Page 3; 10th October 1913, Page 3; 24th October 1913, Page 7 & 14th November 1913, Page 8.

Part Six: The Works of William Hunter Armstrong

1. 'Come all ye bold miners: Ballads & Songs of the Coalfields.' Compiled by A.L. Lloyd. Revised Edition 1978, Page 363.

2. 'General History of Tanfield Lea and Neighbourhood' by Tanfield Lea Women's Institute, February 1960, Page 46.

3. 'The Story of Tanfield and Beamish' by Frederick J. Wade, February 1968, Page 82.

4. 'Stanley News' dated 18th February 1943, Page 1.

5. 'Stanley News' dated 25th February 1943, Page 1.

6. Notes by A.L. Lloyd, Folklorist of an interview with William Hunter Armstrong which are held with numerous papers of Lloyd in the Special Collections at Goldsmiths College, New Cross – part of London University. Ref. Code: GB2603 Lloyd.

7. 'Come all ye bold miners: Ballads & Songs of the Coalfields'. Compiled by A.L. Lloyd. Revised Edition 1978, Page 293.

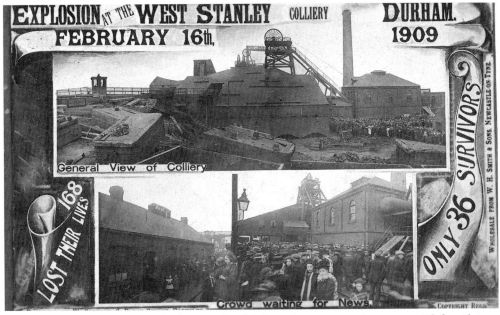

This memorial postcard shows the high price some pitmen paid for the pursuit of coal.

Also available from Summerhill Books

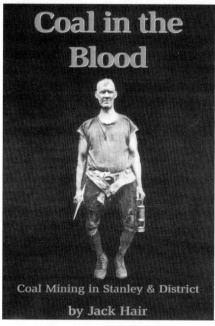

Coal in the Blood
Coal Mining in
Stanley & District

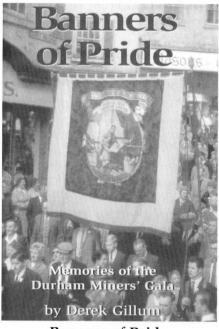

Banners of Pride
Memories of the
Durham Miners' Gala

Summerhill Books

Summerhill Books publishes local
history books in Northumberland,
Durham and Tyneside.

To receive a free catalogue send a
SAE envelope to:

Summerhill Books
PO Box 1210, Newcastle NE99 4AH

or email:
summerhillbooks@yahoo.co.uk

or visit our website to view the full
range of titles

www.summerhillbooks.co.uk

Postage and packaging is
FREE for all UK orders.

Wallsend Best
A Personal Experience of the
Rising Sun Colliery

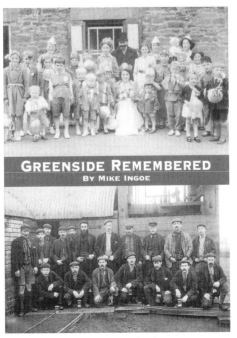

Greenside Remembered

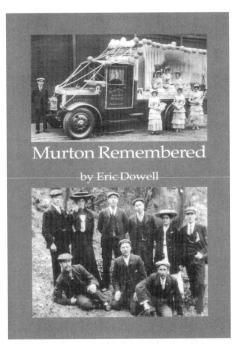

Murton Remembered

Thanks For The Memories
(Fence Houses, Lambton,
Burnmoor, Chilton Moor,
Dubmire & Bankhead)

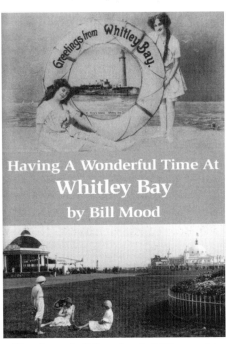

**Having A Wonderful Time At
Whitley Bay**

BIBLIOGRAPHY

A Beuk of the Sangs of Tommy Armstrong, The Pitman's Poet by Conrad Bladey of Hutman Productions – 2003.

Come all ye bold miners: Ballads & Songs of the Coalfields compiled by A.L. Lloyd – 1952. Also revised edition 1978.

Das Leben Eines Englischen Bergarbeitersangers in Deutches Jahrbuch fur Volkskunde, 1964, Band 10, Teil 1, pages 133-143

Folk Song in England by A.L. Lloyd – 1967.

General History of Tanfield Lea & Neighbourhood by Tanfield Lea Women's Institute – 1960.

Heritage and Harmony: MA History Dissertation of Judith Anne Murphy – 2003.

Jubilee History of West Stanley Co-operative Society 1876-1926 by John W. White, JP and Robert Simpson, FCRA

Miners of Northumberland and Durham – by Richard Fynes, 1873.

My Ancestor was a Coalminer by David Tonks – 2002.

Pitmatic: The Talk of the North East Coalfield compiled by Bill Griffiths.

Polisses and Candymen: The Complete Works of Tommy Armstrong – The Pitman Poet edited by Ross Forbes and published by Tommy Armstrong Memorial Trust, Consett, 1987.

The Story of Tanfield and Beamish by Frederick J. Wade – February 1968.

The Story of West Stanley – by Frederick J. Wade – December 1956.

BACK COVER:

Top photograph: William Hunter Armstrong – 1923.

Bottom photograph: Tanfield Lea Lodge Banner of the National Union of Mineworkers.